200 SENSATIONAL STEP-BY-STEP
DESSERTS

MOUTHWATERING RECIPES FOR DELECTABLE DISHES
SHOWN IN MORE THAN 750 GLORIOUS PHOTOGRAPHS

contributing editor: rosemary wilkinson

JG
PRESS

Published by World Publications Group, Inc.
140 Laurel Street, East Bridgewater, MA 02333
www.wrldpub.net

Produced by Anness Publishing Ltd
Hermes House, 88–89 Blackfriars Road
London SE1 8HA
tel. 020 7401 2077; fax 020 7633 9499
www.annesspublishing.com

If you like the images in this book and would like to investigate using them for publishing, promotions
or advertising, please visit our website www.practicalpictures.com for more information.

Publisher: Joanna Lorenz
Copy Editor: Karen Douthwaite
Designer: Bill Mason
Recipes: Carla Capalbo, Francis Cleary, Deh-Ta Hsiung, Norma MacMillan,
Laura Washburn and Stephen Wheeler
Photographers: Karl Adamson, Edward Allwright, Steve Baxter, James Duncan,
Amanda Heywood, Don Last and Michael Michaels
Food for Photography: Carla Capalbo, Francis Cleary, Carole Handslip, Jane Hartshorn,
Wendy Lee, Jane Stevenson and Elizabeth Wolf Cohen
Stylists: Carla Capalbo, Madeleine Brehaut, Diana Civil, Amanda Heywood,
Maria Kelly, Blake Minton, Kirsty Rawlings and Fiona Tillett

ETHICAL TRADING POLICY

Because of our ongoing ecological investment programme, you, as our customer, can have the pleasure and reassurance
of knowing that a tree is being cultivated on your behalf to naturally replace the materials used to make the book
you are holding. For further information about this scheme, go to www.annesspublishing.com/trees

A CIP catalogue record for this book is available from the British Library.

ISBN-10: 1-57215-486-1
ISBN-13: 978-1-57215-486-5

Printed and bound in China

Previously published as *Desserts*

NOTES
Standard spoon and cup measures are level.

Large eggs are used unless otherwise stated.

Electric oven temperatures in this book are for conventional ovens. When using a fan oven, the temperature will
probably need to be reduced by about 20–40°F. Since ovens vary, you should check with your
manufacturer's instruction book for guidance.

Front cover shows Chocolate Chip and Banana Pudding – for recipe, see page 81.

CONTENTS

~

Introduction

DESSERT RECIPES CAN RANGE from the lightest sorbet to the most substantial steamed chocolate pudding, so there are several decisions to be made when planning a menu. Your choice of what to serve will be influenced by the season and the occasion. If you are serving a filling main course you will invariably choose a light or fruity dessert to follow it, or if you plan to make a rich, creamy dessert you will deliberately pick a light main course. The time you have for preparation will also affect your choice. Many of the desserts in this selection can be made a day or two in advance, others can be started early in the day and finished off just before you eat, while frozen desserts and ice creams can be made weeks in advance and will be ready to serve whenever you need them. If you are planning a festive meal or entertaining a large number of people, make sure you leave plenty of time for preparation, choose one of the desserts that can be made in advance and do at least some of the work for the other courses earlier in the day. That way you *and* your guests can enjoy the meal.

All the recipes have clear step-by-step instructions, so that even the traditional chef's nightmares, such as soufflés and roulades, will be easy to make and look and taste delicious. It helps to read the whole recipe through before you start, too, so that you understand the steps involved. In this introductory section you'll find special tips and techniques and some basic recipes, plus helpful hints on preparing the pastry and decorations for pies and tarts.

Black Forest Torte, Crème Caramel, Apple Pie – you will find all the old favorites here, alongside some more unusual recipes which are destined to become your new favorites. Most of the recipes are based on a family of four people, but they can easily be halved for two or doubled for eight. There are chapters on desserts both cold and hot, quick and easy, low-calorie and extra-rich and many more, to make sure you serve a best-ever dessert for every occasion.

Making Pie Crust

A meltingly crisp, crumbly pastry sets off any filling to perfection, whether sweet or savory. The fat content of the pastry dough can be made up of half butter or margarine and half white vegetable shortening or with all one kind of fat.

INGREDIENTS

For a 9-inch pastry shell

2 cups all-purpose flour

¼ teaspoon salt

8 tablespoons fat, chilled and diced

1 Sift the flour and salt into a bowl. Add the fat. Rub it into the flour with your fingertips until the mixture is crumbly.

2 Sprinkle 3 tablespoons ice water over the mixture. With a fork, toss gently to mix and moisten it.

3 Press the dough into a ball. If it is too dry to hold together, gradually add another 1 tablespoon ice water.

4 Wrap the ball of dough with plastic wrap or waxed paper and chill it for at least 30 minutes.

5 To make pastry in a food processor: Combine the flour, salt and cubed cold fat in the work bowl. Process, turning the machine on and off, just until the mixture is crumbly. Add 3–4 tablespoons ice water and process again briefly – just until the dough starts to pull away from the sides of the bowl. It should still look crumbly. Remove the dough from the bowl and gather it into a ball. Wrap and chill.

PIE CRUST VARIATIONS

For Nut Pie Crust

Add ¼ cup finely chopped walnuts or pecans to the flour mixture.

For Rich Pie Crust

Use 2 cups flour and ¾ cup fat (preferably all butter), plus 1 tablespoon superfine sugar if making a sweet pie. Bind with 1 egg yolk and 2–3 tablespoons water.

For a Two-crust Pie

Increase the proportions for these pastries by 50%. Thus the amounts needed for basic pie crust pastry are: 3 cups flour, ½ teaspoon salt, ¾ cup fat, 5–6 tablespoons water.

PASTRY MAKING TIPS

It helps if the fat is cold and firm, particularly if making the dough in a food processor. Cold fat has less chance of warming and softening too much when it is being rubbed into the flour, resulting in an oily pastry. Use block margarine rather than the whipped type for the same reason.

When rubbing the fat into the flour, if it begins to soften and feel oily, put the bowl in the fridge to chill for 20–30 minutes. Then continue to make the dough.

Liquids used should be ice-cold so they will not soften or melt the fat.

Take care when adding the water: Start with the smaller amount (added all at once, not in a dribble), and add more only if the mixture will not come together into a dough. Too much water will make the dough difficult to handle and will result in tough pastry.

When gathering the mixture together into a ball of dough, handle it as little as possible: Overworked dough will again produce a tough pastry.

To avoid shrinkage, chill the pastry dough before rolling out and baking. This 'resting time' will allow any elasticity developed during mixing to relax.

Making French Tart Pastry

The pastry for tarts is made with butter or margarine, giving a rich and crumbly result. The more fat used, the richer the pastry will be – almost like a cookie dough – and the harder to roll out. If you have difficulty rolling it, you can press it into the pan instead, or roll it out between sheets of plastic wrap. Tart pastry, like pie crust, can be made by hand or in a food processor. Tips for making, handling and using pie crust pastry apply equally to this type of pastry.

INGREDIENTS

For a 9-inch tart shell

1¾ cups all-purpose flour

½ teaspoon salt

½ cup butter or margarine, chilled

1 egg yolk

¼ teaspoon lemon juice

1 Sift the flour and salt into a bowl. Add the butter or margarine. Rub into the flour until the mixture resembles fine bread crumbs.

2 In a small bowl, mix the egg yolk, lemon juice and 2 tablespoons ice water. Add to the flour mixture. With a fork, toss gently to mix and moisten.

3 Press the dough into a rough ball. If it is too dry to come together, add 1 tablespoon of water. Turn onto the work surface or a pastry board.

4 With the heel of your hand, push small portions of dough away from you, smearing them on the surface.

5 Continue mixing the dough in this way until it feels pliable and can be peeled easily off the work surface or pastry board.

6 Press the dough into a smooth ball. Wrap in plastic wrap and chill for at least 30 minutes.

TART PASTRY VARIATIONS

For Sweet Tart Pastry
Reduce the amount of salt to ¼ teaspoon and add 1 tablespoon superfine sugar with the flour.

For Rich Tart Pastry
Use 1¾ cups flour, ½ teaspoon salt, 10 tablespoons butter, 2 egg yolks, and 1–2 tablespoons water.

For Rich Sweet Tart Pastry
Make rich tart pastry, adding 3 tablespoons superfine sugar with the flour and, if desired, ½ teaspoon vanilla extract with the egg yolks.

Making Choux Pastry

Unlike other pastries, where the fat is rubbed into the flour, with choux pastry the butter is melted with water and then the flour is added, followed by eggs. The result is more of a paste than a pastry. It is easy to make, but care must be taken in measuring the ingredients.

INGREDIENTS

For 18 profiteroles or 12 éclairs

½ cup butter, cut into small pieces

2 teaspoons superfine sugar (optional)

¼ teaspoon salt

1¼ cups all-purpose flour

4 eggs, beaten

1 egg, beaten with 1 teaspoon cold water, for glaze

1 Preheat the oven to 425°F. Combine the butter, sugar, if using, salt and 1 cup water in a large heavy saucepan. Bring to a boil over medium high heat, stirring occasionally.

2 As soon as the mixture is boiling, remove the pan from the heat. Add the flour all at once and beat vigorously with a wooden spoon to mix the flour smoothly into the liquid.

3 Return the pan to medium heat and cook, stirring, until the mixture forms a ball, pulling away from the side of the pan. This will take about 1 minute. Remove from the heat again and let cool for 3–5 minutes.

4 Add a little of the beaten eggs and beat well to incorporate. Add a little more egg and beat in well. Continue beating in the eggs until the mixture becomes a smooth and shiny paste.

5 While still warm, shape choux puffs, éclairs, profiteroles or rings on a baking sheet lined with parchment paper.

6 Glaze with 1 egg beaten with 1 teaspoon cold water. Put into the preheated oven, then reduce the heat to 400°F. Bake until puffed and golden brown.

SHAPING CHOUX PASTRY

For Large Puffs
Use two large spoons dipped in water. Drop the paste in 2–2½-inch wide mounds on the paper-lined baking sheet, leaving 1½ inches between each. Neaten the mounds as much as possible. Alternatively, for well-shaped puffs, pipe the paste using a pastry bag fitted with a ¾-inch plain nozzle.

For Profiteroles
Use two small spoons or a pastry bag fitted with a ½-inch nozzle and shape 1-inch mounds.

For Éclairs
Use a pastry bag fitted with a ¾-inch nozzle. Pipe strips 4–5 inches long.

For a Ring
Draw a 12-inch circle on the paper. Spoon the paste in large mounds on the circle to make a ring. Or pipe two rings around the circle and a third on top.

BAKING TIMES FOR CHOUX PASTRY	
Large puffs and éclairs	30–35 minutes
Profiteroles	20–25 minutes
Rings	40–45 minutes

Rolling Out and Lining a Pie Pan

A neat pastry shell that doesn't distort or shrink in baking is what you want. The key to success is handling the dough gently. Use the method here to line a round pie or tart pan that is about 2 inches deep.

Remove the chilled dough from the fridge and let it soften slightly at room temperature. Unwrap and put it on a lightly floured surface. Flatten the dough into a neat, round circle. Lightly flour the rolling pin.

1 Using even pressure, start rolling out the dough, working from the center to the edge each time and easing the pressure slightly as you reach the edge.

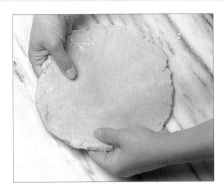

2 Lift up the dough and give it a quarter turn from time to time during the rolling. This will prevent the dough from sticking to the surface, and will help keep the thickness even.

3 Continue rolling out until the dough circle is about 2 inches larger all around than the pan. It should be about ⅛ inch thick.

4 Put the rolling pin on the dough, near one side of the circle. Fold the outside edge of the dough over the pin, then roll the pin over the dough to wrap the dough round it. Do this gently and loosely.

5 Hold the pin over the pan and gently unroll the dough so it drapes into the pan, centering it as much as possible.

6 With your fingertips, lift and ease the dough into the pan, gently pressing it over the bottom and up the side. Turn excess dough over the rim and trim it with a knife or scissors, depending on the edge to be made.

Finishing the Edge

1 *For a forked edge:* Trim the dough even with the rim and press it flat. Firmly and evenly press the prongs of a fork all around the edge. If the fork sticks, dip it in flour every so often.

2 *For a crimped edge:* Trim the dough to leave an overhang of about ½ inch all around. Fold the extra dough under. Put the knuckle or tip of the index finger of one of your hands inside the edge, pointing directly out. With the thumb and index finger of your other hand, pinch the dough edge around your index finger into a "V" shape. Continue all the way around the edge.

3 *For a ruffled edge:* Trim the dough to leave an overhang of about ½ inch all around. Fold the extra dough under. Hold the thumb and index finger of one of your hands about 1 inch apart, inside the edge, pointing directly out. With the index finger of your other hand, gently pull the dough between them, to the end of the rim. Continue this all the way around the edge.

4 *For a cutout edge:* Trim the dough even with the rim and press it flat on the rim. With a small cookie cutter, cut out decorative shapes from the dough trimmings. Moisten the edge of the pastry case and press the cutouts in place, overlapping them slightly if you like.

5 *For a ribbon edge:* Trim the dough even with the rim and press it flat. Cut long strips about ¾ inch wide from the dough trimmings. Moisten the edge and press one end of a strip onto it. Twist the strip gently and press it onto the edge again. Continue all the way around the edge.

Preparing Fresh Fruit

PEELING AND TRIMMING FRUIT

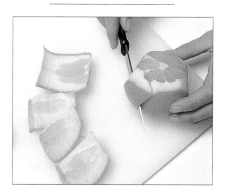

Citrus Fruit

To peel completely: Cut a slice from the top and from the base. Set the fruit base down on a work surface. Using a small, sharp knife, cut off the peel lengthwise in thick strips. Remove the colored rind and all the white pith (which has a bitter taste). Cut, following the curve of the fruit.

To remove rind: Use a vegetable peeler to peel off the rind in wide strips, taking none of the white pith. Use these strips whole or cut them into fine shreds with a sharp knife, according to recipe directions. Or rub the fruit against the fine holes of a metal grater, turning the fruit so you take just the colored rind and not the white pith. Or use a special tool, called a citrus zester, to take fine threads of rind. (Finely chop the threads as an alternative method to grating.)

Kiwi Fruit

Follow the citrus fruit technique, taking off the peel in thin, lengthwise strips.

Apples, pears, quinces, mangoes, papayas

Use a small, sharp knife or a vegetable peeler. Take off the peel in long strips, as thinly as possible.

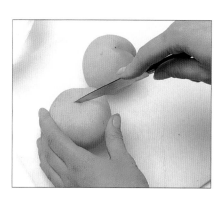

Peaches, apricots

Cut a cross in the base. Immerse the fruit in boiling water. Let stand for 10–30 seconds (according to ripeness), then drain and immerse in ice water. The skin should slip off easily.

Pineapple

Cut off the leafy crown. Cut a slice from the base and set the pineapple upright. With a sharp knife, cut off the peel lengthwise, cutting thickly to remove the brown "eyes" with it.

Bananas, lychees, avocados

Make a small cut and remove the peel with your fingers.

Passion Fruit, pomegranates

Cut in half, or cut a slice off the top. With a spoon, scoop the flesh and seeds into a bowl.

Star Fruit (carambola)

Trim off the tough, darkened edges of the five segments.

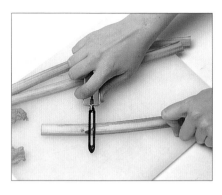

Rhubarb
Cut off the leaves and discard them (they are poisonous). Peel off any tough skin.

Fresh Currants (red, black, white)
Pull each cluster through the prongs of a fork to remove the currants from the stalks.

Fresh Dates
Squeeze gently at the stalk end to remove the rather tough skin.

CORING AND PITTING OR SEEDING FRUIT

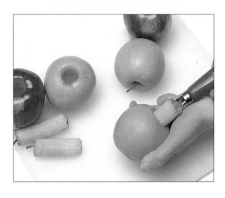

Apples, pears, quinces
For whole fruit: Use an apple corer to remove the whole core from stalk end to base. Alternatively, working up from the base, use a melon baller to cut out the core. Leave the stalk end intact.

For halves: Use a melon baller to scoop out the core. Cut out the stalk and base using a small sharp knife.
For quarters: Cut out the stalk and core with a serrated knife.

Citrus Fruit
With the tip of a pointed knife, lever out seeds from slices or segments.

Cherries
Use a cherry pitter for the neatest results.

Peaches, apricots, nectarines, plums
Cut the fruit in half, cutting around the indentation. Twist the halves apart. Lift out the pit, or lever it out with the tip of a sharp knife.

Fresh Dates
Cut the fruit lengthwise in half and lift out the pit. Or, if the fruit is to be used whole, cut in from the stalk end with a thin-bladed knife to loosen the pit, then remove it.

Mangoes

Cut lengthwise on either side of the large, flat pit in the center. Curve the cut slightly to follow the shape of the pit. Cut the flesh from the two thin ends of the pit.

Papayas, melons

Cut the fruit in half. Scoop out the seeds from the central hollow, then scrape away any fibers.

Pineapple

For spears and wedges: Cut out the core neatly with a sharp knife.
For rings: Cut out the core with a small pastry cutter.

Gooseberries

Use scissors to trim off the stalk and flower ends.

Grapes

Cut the fruit lengthwise in half. Use a small knife to lever out the seeds. Alternatively, use the curved end of a sterilized hair pin.

Star Fruit (carambola), watermelon

With the tip of a pointed knife, lever out seeds from slices.

Strawberries

Use a special huller to remove leafy green top and central core. Or cut these out with a small, sharp knife.

Avocado

Cut the fruit in half lengthwise. Stick the tip of a sharp knife into the pit and lever it out without damaging the surrounding flesh.

Apples, quinces

For rings: Remove the core and seeds with an apple corer. Set the fruit on its side and cut across into thick or thin rings, as required.

For slices: Cut the fruit in half and remove core and seeds with a melon baller. Set one half cut side down and cut it across into neat slices, thick or thin according to recipe directions. Or cut the fruit into quarters and remove core and seeds with a knife. Cut lengthwise into neat slices.

Pears

For fans: Cut the fruit in half and remove the core and seeds with a melon baller. Set one half cut side down and cut lengthwise into thin slices, not cutting all the way through at the stalk end. Gently fan out the slices so they are overlapping each other evenly. Transfer the pear fan to a plate or pastry shell using a spatula.
For slices: Follow apple technique.

Chocolate Fudge Sauce

A real treat if you're not counting calories. Fabulous with scoops of vanilla ice cream.

Serves 6

⅔ cup heavy cream

¼ cup butter

¼ cup granulated sugar

6 ounces semisweet chocolate

2 tablespoons brandy

VARIATIONS

White Chocolate and Orange Sauce

3 tablespoons superfine sugar, to replace granulated sugar

finely grated rind of 1 orange

6 ounces white chocolate, to replace semisweet chocolate

2 tablespoons orange liqueur, to replace brandy

Coffee Chocolate Fudge

¼ cup light brown sugar, to replace granulated sugar

2 tablespoons coffee liqueur or dark rum, to replace brandy

1 tablespoon coffee extract

1 Heat the cream with the butter and sugar in the top of a double boiler or in a heatproof bowl over a saucepan of hot water. Stir until smooth, then cool.

2 Break the chocolate into the cream. Stir until it is melted and thoroughly combined.

3 Stir in the brandy a little at a time, then cool to room temperature.

4 For the White Chocolate and Orange Sauce, heat the cream and butter with the sugar and orange rind in the top of a double boiler, until dissolved. Follow the recipe to the end, but use white chocolate and orange liqueur instead.

5 For the Coffee Chocolate Fudge, follow the recipe, using light brown sugar and coffee liqueur or rum. Stir in the coffee extract at the end.

6 Serve the sauce over cream-filled profiteroles, and serve any that is left over separately.

Glossy Chocolate Sauce

Delicious poured over ice cream or on hot or cold desserts, this sauce also freezes well. Pour into a freezer-proof container, seal and keep for up to three months. Thaw at room temperature.

Serves 6

½ cup superfine sugar

6 ounces semisweet chocolate, broken into squares

2 tablespoons unsalted butter

2 tablespoons brandy or orange juice

1 Place the sugar and ¼ cup water in a saucepan and heat gently, stirring occasionally, until the sugar has dissolved.

2 Stir in the chocolate, a few squares at a time, until melted, then add the butter in the same way. Do not let the sauce boil. Stir in the brandy or orange juice and serve warm.

COLD
DESSERTS

~

Boodles Orange Fool

This British dessert became the spe-cialty of Boodles Club, a gentlemen's club in London's St. James's.

INGREDIENTS

Serves 4

4 trifle sponge cakes, cubed

1¼ cups heavy cream

2–4 tablespoons superfine sugar

grated rind and juice of 2 oranges

grated rind and juice of 1 lemon

orange and lemon slices and rind,
    to decorate

1 Line the bottom and halfway up the sides of a large glass serving bowl or china dish with the cubed trifle sponge cakes.

2 Whip the cream with the sugar until it starts to thicken, then gradually whip in the fruit juices, adding the fruit rinds once most of the juices have been incorporated.

3 Carefully pour the cream mixture into the bowl or dish, taking care not to dislodge the sponge cakes. Cover and chill for 3–4 hours. Serve decorated with orange and lemon slices and rind.

Apricot and Orange Gelatin

A light and refreshing dessert for a summer's day.

INGREDIENTS

Serves 4

12 ounces flavorful fresh ripe
    apricots, pitted

about ⅓ cup granulated sugar

1¼ cups freshly squeezed orange juice

1 tablespoon powdered gelatin

light cream, to serve

finely chopped candied orange peel,
    to decorate

1 Heat the apricots, sugar and ½ cup of the orange juice, stirring until the sugar has dissolved. Simmer gently until the apricots are tender.

2 Press the apricot mixture through a nylon sieve into a small measuring cup using a spoon.

3 Pour 3 tablespoons of the orange juice into a small heatproof bowl, sprinkle the gelatin over it and let stand for about 5 minutes, until softened.

4 Place the bowl over a saucepan of hot water and heat until the gelatin has dissolved. Slowly pour into the apricot mixture, stirring constantly. Measure up to 2½ cups with the remaining orange juice.

5 Pour the apricot mixture into four individual dishes and chill until set. To serve, pour a thin layer of cream over the surface, and decorate with candied orange peel.

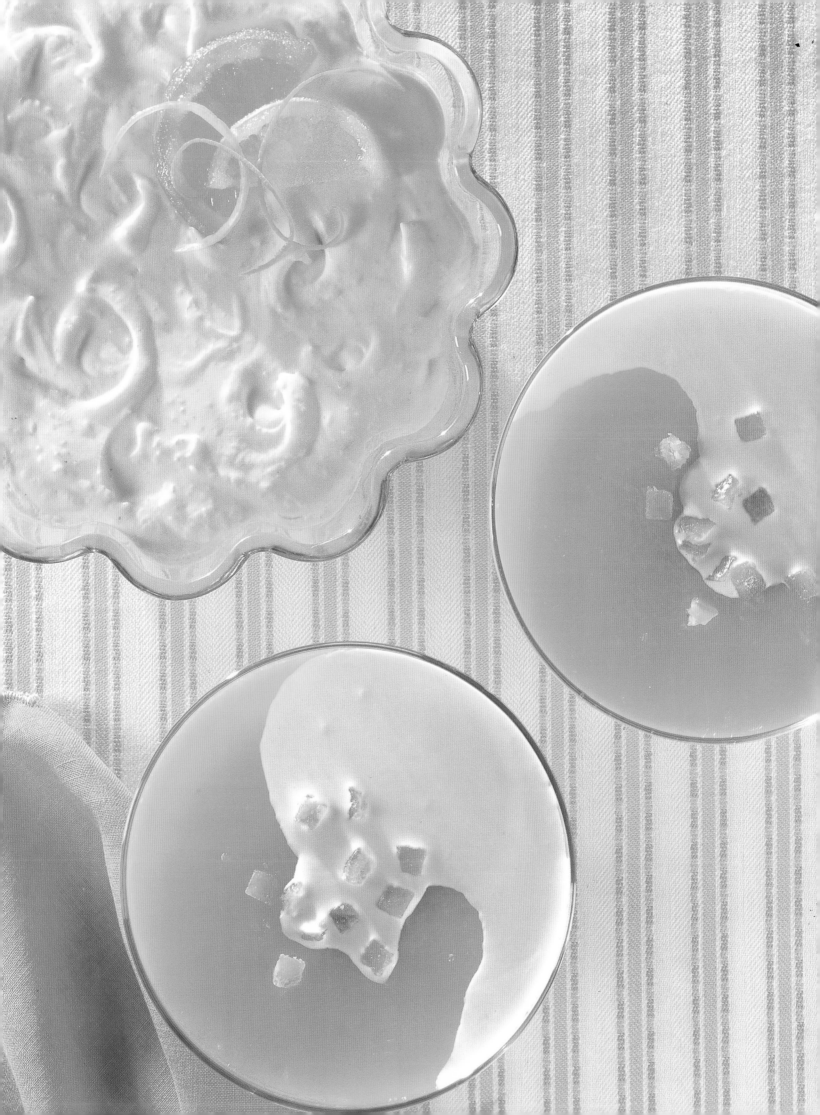

Tangerine Trifle

An unusual variation on a traditional trifle – of course, you can add a little alcohol if you wish.

INGREDIENTS

Serves 4

5 trifle sponges, halved lengthwise

2 tablespoons apricot jam

15–20 macaroons

1 package (5 ounces) tangerine or orange gelatin

1 can (11 ounces) mandarin oranges, drained, reserving juice

2½ cups packaged (or homemade) custard

whipped cream and shreds of orange rind, to decorate

superfine sugar, for sprinkling

1 Spread the halved sponge cakes with apricot jam and arrange in the bottom of a deep serving bowl or glass dish. Sprinkle with the macaroons.

2 Put the gelatin into a heatproof bowl or pan, add the juice from the canned mandarins and dissolve in a pan of hot water or in the microwave. Stir until the liquid clears.

3 Add up to 2½ cups ice cold water, stir well and let cool for up to 30 minutes. Scatter the mandarin oranges over the cakes and macaroons.

4 Pour the gelatin over the mandarin oranges, cake and macaroons and chill for 1 hour.

5 When the gelatin has set, pour the custard smoothly over the top and chill again.

6 When ready to serve, pipe the whipped cream over the custard. Wash the orange rind shreds, sprinkle them with superfine sugar and use to decorate the trifle.

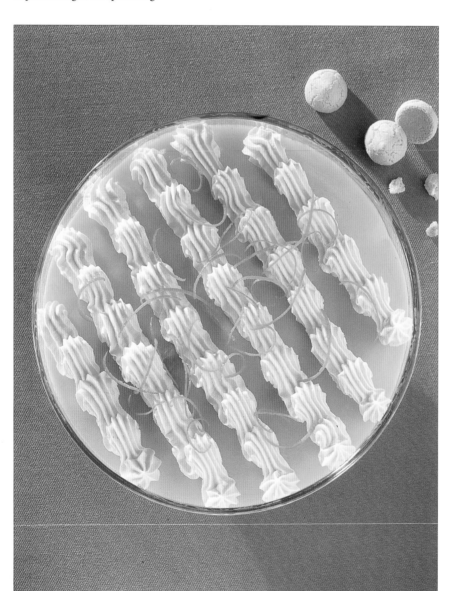

Lemon Soufflé with Blackberries

The simple, fresh taste of cold lemon soufflé combines well with rich blackberry sauce, and the color contrast looks wonderful, too. Blueberries or raspberries make equally delicious alternatives to blackberries.

INGREDIENTS

Serves 6

grated rind of 1 lemon and juice of
  2 lemons
1 envelope powdered gelatin
5 small eggs, separated
¾ cup superfine sugar
few drops vanilla extract
1⅔ cups whipping cream

For the sauce
¾ cup blackberries (fresh or frozen)
2–3 tablespoons superfine sugar
few fresh blackberries and blackberry
  leaves, to decorate

1 Place the lemon juice in a small pan and heat through. Sprinkle on the gelatin and let dissolve or heat further until clear. Let cool.

2 Put the lemon rind, egg yolks, sugar and vanilla in a large bowl and whisk until the mixture is very thick, pale and creamy.

3 Whisk the egg whites until stiff and almost peaked. Whip the cream until stiff.

4 Stir the gelatin mixture into the yolks, then fold in the whipped cream and then the egg whites. Transfer into a 6-cup soufflé dish and freeze for about 2 hours.

5 To make the sauce, place the blackberries in a pan with the sugar and cook for 4–6 minutes, until the juices begin to run and all the sugar has dissolved. Press through a sieve to remove the seeds, then chill.

6 When the soufflé is almost frozen, but still spoonable, scoop or spoon out onto individual plates and serve with the blackberry sauce, decorated with fresh blackberries and blackberry leaves.

Chocolate Mandarin Trifle

Trifle is always a tempting treat, but when a rich chocolate and mascarpone custard is combined with amaretto and mandarin oranges, it becomes irresistible.

INGREDIENTS

Serves 6–8

4 trifle sponges

14 amaretti or almond cookies

¼ cup Amaretto di Saronno or sweet sherry

8 mandarin oranges

For the custard

7 ounces semisweet chocolate, broken into squares

2 tablespoons cornstarch or custard powder

2 tablespoons superfine sugar

2 egg yolks

1 cup milk

generous 1 cup mascarpone

For the topping

generous 1 cup fromage frais or cream cheese

chocolate shapes

mandarin slices

1 Break up the trifle sponges and place them in a large glass serving dish. Crumble the amaretti cookies over them and then sprinkle with amaretto or sweet sherry.

2 Squeeze the juice from 2 of the mandarins and sprinkle into the dish. Segment the rest and put them in the dish.

3 Make the custard. Melt the chocolate in a heatproof bowl over hot water. In a separate bowl, mix the cornstarch, sugar and egg yolks to a smooth paste.

4 Heat the milk in a small saucepan until almost boiling, then pour in a steady stream onto the egg yolk mixture, stirring constantly. Return to the clean pan and stir over low heat until the custard has thickened slightly and is smooth.

5 Stir in the mascarpone until melted, then add the melted chocolate, mixing it thoroughly. Spread evenly over the trifle, cool, then chill until set.

6 To finish, spread the fromage frais over the custard, then decorate with chocolate shapes and the remaining mandarin slices just before serving.

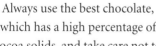

COOK'S TIP

Always use the best chocolate, which has a high percentage of cocoa solids, and take care not to overheat the chocolate when melting as it will lose its gloss and look grainy.

Lime Sherbet

This light, refreshing sherbet is a good dessert to serve after a substantial main course.

INGREDIENTS

Serves 4

1¼ cups granulated sugar

grated rind of 1 lime

¾ cup freshly squeezed lime juice

1–2 tablespoons fresh lemon juice

confectioners' sugar, to taste

slivers of lime rind, to decorate

1 In a small heavy saucepan, dissolve the granulated sugar in 2½ cups of water, without stirring, over medium heat. When the sugar has dissolved, boil for 5-6 minutes. Remove from the heat and let cool.

2 Combine the cooled sugar syrup and lime rind and juice in a measuring cup or bowl. Stir well. Taste and adjust the flavor by adding lemon juice or some confectioners' sugar, if necessary. Do not over-sweeten.

3 Freeze the mixture in an ice cream maker, following the manufacturer's instructions.

4 If you do not have an ice cream maker, pour the mixture into a metal or plastic freezer container and freeze until softly set, about 3 hours.

5 Remove from the container and chop coarsely into 3-inch pieces. Place in a food processor and process until smooth. Return the mixture to the freezer container and freeze again until set. Repeat this freezing and chopping process two or three times, until a smooth consistency is obtained.

6 Serve in scoops, decorated with slivers of lime rind.

COOK'S TIP

If using an ice cream maker for these sherbets, check the manufacturer's instructions to find out the freezing capacity. If necessary, halve the recipe quantities.

Gooseberry and Elderflower Cream

When elderflowers are in season, instead of using the cordial, cook two to three elderflower heads with the gooseberries.

INGREDIENTS

Serves 4

1¼ pounds gooseberries, ends removed

1¼ cups heavy cream

1 cup confectioners' sugar, to taste

2 tablespoons elderflower cordial or orange flower water (optional)

mint sprigs, to decorate

almond cookies, to serve

2 Beat the cream until soft peaks form, then fold in half of the gooseberries. Sweeten and add elderflower cordial or orange flower water, if using. Sweeten the remaining gooseberries.

3 Layer the cream mixture and the crushed gooseberries in four dessert dishes or tall glasses, then cover and chill. Decorate with mint sprigs and serve accompanied by almond cookies.

1 Place the gooseberries in a heavy saucepan, cover and cook over low heat, shaking the pan occasionally, until the gooseberries are tender. Put the gooseberries into a bowl, crush them, then let cool completely.

COOK'S TIP

If preferred, the cooked gooseberries can be puréed and strained. An equivalent quantity of real custard can replace the cream.

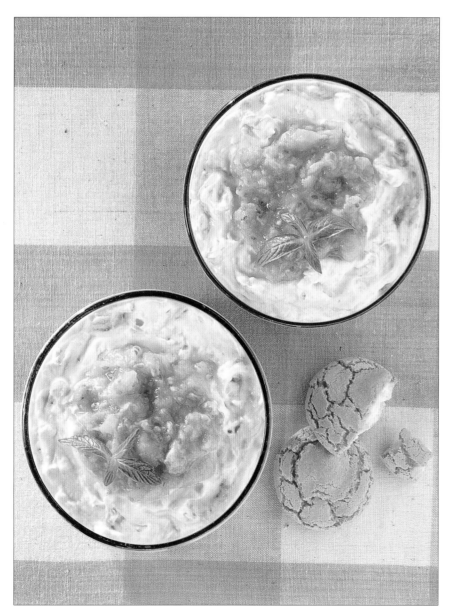

Apricots with Orange Cream

Mascarpone is a very rich cream cheese made from thick Lombardy cream. It is delicious flavored with orange as a topping for these poached, chilled apricots.

INGREDIENTS

Serves 4

2 cups dried apricots

strip of orange peel

1 cinnamon stick

3 tablespoons superfine sugar

⅔ cup sweet dessert wine (such as sweet Californian Muscat)

½ cup mascarpone

3 tablespoons orange juice

pinch of ground cinnamon and fresh mint sprig, to decorate

1 Place the apricots, orange peel, cinnamon stick and 1 tablespoon of the sugar in a pan and cover with 2 cups cold water. Bring to a boil, cover and simmer gently for 25 minutes, until the fruit is tender.

2 Remove from the heat and stir in the dessert wine. Let stand until cold, then chill for at least 3–4 hours or overnight.

3 Combine the mascarpone, orange juice and the remaining sugar in a bowl and beat well until smooth, then chill.

4 Just before serving, remove the cinnamon stick and orange peel, and serve with a spoonful of the orange cream sprinkled with cinnamon and decorated with a sprig of fresh mint.

Rhubarb and Orange Fool

Perhaps this traditional English pudding got its name because it is so easy to make that even a "fool" can attempt it.

INGREDIENTS

Serves 4

2 tablespoons orange juice

1 teaspoon finely shredded orange rind

2 pounds (about 10–12 stems) rhubarb, chopped

1 tablespoon red currant jelly

3 tablespoons superfine sugar

⅔ cup ready-to-serve thick and creamy custard

⅔ cup heavy cream, whipped

cookies, to serve

1 Place the orange juice and rind, the rhubarb, red currant jelly and sugar in a saucepan. Cover and simmer gently for about 8 minutes, stirring occasionally, until the rhubarb is just tender, but not mushy.

2 Remove the pan from the heat, transfer the rhubarb to a bowl and let cool completely.

3 Drain the cooled rhubarb to remove some of the liquid. Reserve a few pieces of the rhubarb and a little orange rind for decoration. Purée the remaining rhubarb in a food processor or blender, or press through a sieve.

4 Stir the custard into the purée, then fold in the whipped cream. Spoon the fool into individual bowls, cover and chill. Just before serving, top with the reserved fruit and rind. Serve with crisp cookies.

Cherry Syllabub

This recipe follows the style of the earliest syllabubs from the sixteenth and seventeenth centuries, producing a frothy, creamy layer over a liquid one.

Serves 4

8 ounces ripe dark cherries, pitted and chopped

2 tablespoons kirsch

2 egg whites

scant ½ cup superfine sugar

2 tablespoons lemon juice

⅔ cup sweet white wine

1¼ cups heavy cream

1 Divide the chopped cherries among six tall dessert glasses and sprinkle with the kirsch.

2 In a clean bowl, whisk the egg whites until stiff. Gently fold in the sugar, lemon juice and wine.

3 In a separate bowl (but using the same whisk), lightly beat the cream, then fold into the egg white mixture.

4 Spoon the cream mixture over the cherries, then chill overnight.

Rose Petal Cream

This is an old-fashioned junket that is set with rennet – don't move it while it is setting, otherwise it will separate.

Serves 4

2½ cups milk

3 tablespoons superfine sugar

several drops triple-strength rosewater

2 teaspoons rennet

¼ cup heavy cream

sugared rose petals, to decorate (optional)

1 Gently heat the milk and 2 tablespoons of the sugar, stirring constantly, until the sugar has melted and the temperature reaches 98.6°F, or when the milk feels lukewarm.

2 Stir rosewater to taste into the milk, then remove the pan from the heat before stirring in the rennet.

3 Pour the milk into a serving dish and leave undisturbed for 2–3 hours, until the junket has set.

4 Stir the remaining sugar into the cream, then carefully spoon over the junket. Decorate with sugared rose petals, if desired.

COOK'S TIP

Only use rose petals taken from bushes that have not been sprayed with chemicals of any kind.

Raspberry Meringue Gâteau

A rich, hazelnut meringue sandwiched with whipped cream and raspberries makes an irresistible dessert for a special occasion.

Serves 6

4 egg whites

1 cup superfine sugar

a few drops vanilla extract

1 teaspoon distilled malt vinegar

1 cup roasted and chopped hazelnuts, ground

1¼ cups heavy cream

2 cups raspberries

confectioners' sugar, for dusting

mint sprigs, to decorate

For the sauce

1⅓ cups raspberries

3–4 tablespoons confectioners' sugar, sifted

1 tablespoon orange liqueur

1 Preheat the oven to 350°F. Grease two 8-inch pans and line the bottoms with waxed paper.

2 Whisk the egg whites in a large bowl until they hold stiff peaks, then gradually whisk in the superfine sugar one tablespoon at a time, whisking after each addition.

COOK'S TIP

You can buy roasted, chopped hazelnuts in supermarkets. Otherwise toast whole hazelnuts under the broiler and rub off the flaky skins, using a clean dish-towel. To chop finely, process in a blender or food processor for a few moments.

3 Continue whisking the meringue mixture for a minute of two, until very stiff, then fold in the vanilla extract, vinegar and ground hazelnuts.

4 Divide the meringue mixture between the prepared cake pans and spread level. Bake for 50–60 minutes, until crisp. Remove the meringues from the pans and let them cool on a wire rack.

5 While the meringues are cooling, make the sauce. Process the raspberries with the confectioners' sugar and orange liqueur in a blender or food processor, then press the purée through a fine sieve to remove any seeds. Chill the sauce until ready to serve.

6 Whip the cream until it forms soft peaks, then gently fold in the raspberries. Sandwich the meringue rounds together with the raspberry cream.

7 Dust the top of the gâteau with confectioners' sugar. Decorate with mint sprigs and serve with the raspberry sauce.

VARIATION

Fresh red currants make a good alternative to raspberries. Pick over the fruit, then pull each sprig gently through the prongs of a fork to release the red currants. Add them to the whipped cream with a little confectioners' sugar, to taste.

Creole Ambrosia

A refreshing cold fruit dessert that can be made at any time of the year.

Serves 6

6 oranges

1 coconut

2 tablespoons superfine sugar

1 Peel the oranges, removing all white pith, then slice thinly, picking out seeds with the point of a knife. Do this on a plate to catch the juice.

2 Pierce the "eyes" of the coconut and pour away the liquid, then crack open the coconut with a hammer. (This is best done outside on a stone surface.)

COOK'S TIP

Mangoes instead of oranges make the dessert more exotic but less authentically Creole.

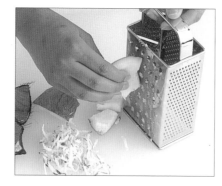

3 Peel the coconut with a sharp knife, then grate half the flesh coarsely, either on a hand grater or on the grating blade of a blender or food processor.

4 Layer the coconut and orange slices in a glass bowl, starting and finishing with the coconut. After each orange layer, sprinkle on a little sugar and pour on some of the reserved orange juice.

5 Let the dessert stand for 2 hours before serving, either at room temperature or, in hot weather, in the refrigerator.

Watermelon Sherbet

A pretty pink sherbet that makes a light and refreshing dessert and could be served before the main course to cleanse the palate at a grand dinner.

INGREDIENTS

Serves 6

2¼ pound piece watermelon

1 cup superfine sugar

juice of 1 lemon

2 egg whites

mint leaves, to decorate

1 Cut the watermelon in wedges, then cut it away from the rind, cubing the flesh and picking out all the seeds.

2 Purée three-quarters of the flesh in a food processor or blender, but mash the last quarter on a plate – this will give the sherbet more texture.

3 Stir the sugar with the lemon juice and ½ cup cold water in a saucepan over very low heat, until the sugar dissolves and the syrup clears.

4 Mix all the watermelon and the syrup in a large bowl and transfer to a freezer container.

5 Freeze for 1–1½ hours, until the edges begin to set. Beat the mixture, return to the freezer and freeze for another hour.

6 When the hour is up, whisk the egg whites to soft peaks. Beat the iced mixture again and fold in the egg whites. Return to the freezer for another hour, then beat once more and freeze firm.

7 Transfer the sherbet from the freezer to the fridge for 20–30 minutes before it is to be served. Serve in scoops, decorated with mint leaves.

Coffee, Vanilla and Chocolate Stripes

This looks really special served in elegant wine glasses and tastes appropriately exquisite.

Serves 6

1½ cups superfine sugar

6 tablespoons cornstarch

3¾ cups milk

3 egg yolks

6 tablespoons unsalted butter, at room temperature

generous 1 tablespoon instant coffee powder

2 teaspoons vanilla extract

2 tablespoons cocoa powder

whipped cream, to serve

1 To make the coffee layer, place ½ cup of the sugar and 2 tablespoons of the cornstarch in a heavy saucepan. Gradually add one-third of the milk, whisking until well blended. Over medium heat, whisk in one of the egg yolks and bring to a boil, whisking. Boil for 1 minute.

2 Remove the pan from the heat. Stir in 2 tablespoons of the butter and the instant coffee powder. Set aside in the pan to cool slightly.

3 Divide the coffee mixture among six wine glasses. Smooth the tops before the mixture sets.

4 Wipe any dribbles on the insides and outsides of the glasses with damp paper towels.

5 To make the vanilla layer, place half of the remaining sugar and cornstarch in a heavy saucepan. Whisk in 1¼ cups of the milk. Over medium heat, whisk in another egg yolk and bring to a boil, whisking. Boil for 1 minute.

6 Remove the pan from the heat and stir in 2 tablespoons of the butter and the vanilla. Let cool slightly, then spoon into the glasses on top of the coffee layer. Smooth the tops and wipe the glasses with paper towels.

7 To make the chocolate layer, place the remaining sugar and cornstarch in a heavy saucepan. Gradually whisk in the remaining milk and continue whisking until blended. Over medium heat, whisk in the last egg yolk and bring to a boil, whisking constantly. Boil for 1 minute. Remove from the heat, and stir in the remaining butter and the cocoa. Let cool slightly, then spoon into the glasses on top of the vanilla layer. Chill until set.

8 Pipe swirls of whipped cream on top of each dessert just before serving.

COOK'S TIP

For a special occasion, prepare the vanilla layer using a fresh vanilla pod. Choose a plump, supple pod and split it down the center with a sharp knife. Add to the mixture with the milk and discard the pod before spooning the mixture into the glasses. The flavor will be more pronounced and the pudding will have pretty brown speckles from the vanilla seeds.

Chocolate Hazelnut Galettes

Chocolate rounds sandwiched with fromage frais. If only all sandwiches looked and tasted this good.

INGREDIENTS

Serves 4

6 ounces semisweet chocolate, broken into squares

3 tablespoons light cream

2 tablespoons flaked hazelnuts

4 ounces white chocolate, broken into squares

¾ cup fromage frais (8% fat) or cream cheese

1 tablespoon dry sherry

¼ cup finely chopped hazelnuts, toasted

physalis (Cape gooseberries), if available, dipped in white chocolate, to decorate

1 Melt the semisweet chocolate in a heatproof bowl over hot water, then remove from the heat and stir in the cream.

2 Draw 12 x 3-inch circles on sheets of waxed paper. Turn the paper over and spread the semisweet chocolate over each marked circle, covering in a thin, even layer. Sprinkle flaked hazelnuts over four of the circles, then let set.

3 Melt the white chocolate in a heatproof bowl over hot water, then stir in the fromage frais and dry sherry. Fold in the chopped, toasted hazelnuts. Let cool until the mixture holds its shape.

4 Remove the chocolate rounds carefully from the paper and sandwich them together in stacks of three, spooning the hazelnut cream between each layer and using the hazelnut-covered rounds on top. Chill before serving.

5 To serve, place the galettes on individual plates and decorate with chocolate-dipped physalis.

COOK'S TIP

The chocolate could be spread over heart shapes instead, for a special Valentine's Day dessert.

Chocolate and Chestnut Pots

Prepared in advance, these are the perfect ending for a dinner party. Remove them from the fridge about 30 minutes before serving, to let them "ripen."

INGREDIENTS

Serves 6

9 ounces semisweet chocolate

¼ cup Madeira

2 tablespoons butter, diced

2 eggs, separated

scant 1 cup unsweetened chestnut purée

crème fraîche or whipped heavy cream,
   to decorate

1 Make a few chocolate curls for decoration, then break the rest of the chocolate into squares and melt it with the Madeira in a saucepan over gentle heat. Remove from the heat and add the butter, a few pieces at a time, stirring until melted and smooth.

COOK'S TIP
〜

If Madeira is not available, use brandy or rum instead. These chocolate pots can be frozen successfully for up to 2 months.

2 Beat the egg yolks quickly into the mixture, then beat in the chestnut purée, mixing until smooth.

3 Whisk the egg whites in a clean, grease-free bowl until stiff. Stir about 1 tablespoon of the whites into the chestnut mixture to lighten it, then fold in the rest smoothly and evenly.

4 Spoon the mixture into six small ramekins and chill until set. Serve the pots topped with a generous spoonful of crème fraîche or whipped heavy cream and decorated with the semisweet chocolate curls.

Coffee Ice Cream with Caramelized Pecans

Coffee and sweetened nuts make a mouthwatering combination.

INGREDIENTS

Serves 4–6

For the ice cream

1¼ cups milk

1 tablespoon raw or light brown sugar

6 tablespoons finely ground coffee or
    1 tablespoon instant coffee granules

1 egg plus 2 yolks

1¼ cups heavy cream

1 tablespoon superfine sugar

For the pecans

1 cup pecan halves

¼ cup dark brown sugar

1 Heat the milk and raw sugar to the boiling point. Remove from the heat and sprinkle on the coffee. Let stand for 2 minutes, then stir, cover and cool.

2 In a heatproof bowl, beat the egg and extra yolks until the mixture is thick and pale.

COOK'S TIP

You can give good-quality bought ice cream a fillip with the same nutty garnish.

3 Strain the coffee mixture into a pan, heat to the boiling point, then pour onto the eggs in a steady stream, beating hard all the time.

4 Set the bowl over a pan of gently simmering water and stir until it thickens. Cool, then chill in the fridge.

5 Whip the cream with the superfine sugar. Fold it into the coffee custard and freeze in a covered container. Beat twice at hourly intervals, then let freeze until firm.

6 To caramelize the nuts, preheat the oven to 350°F. Spread the nuts on a baking sheet in a single layer. Put them into the oven for 10–15 minutes to toast, until they release their fragrance.

7 On the top of the stove, dissolve the brown sugar in 2 tablespoons water in a heavy pan, shaking it around over low heat until the sugar dissolves and the syrup clears.

8 When the syrup begins to bubble, add the toasted pecans and cook for a minute or two over medium heat until the syrup coats and clings to the nuts.

9 Spread the nuts on a lightly oiled baking sheet, separating them with the tip of a knife, and let cool. Store when cold in an airtight tin if they are not to be eaten on the same day.

10 Transfer the ice cream from the freezer to the fridge 30 minutes before scooping it into portions and serving with caramelized pecans.

White Chocolate Parfait

Everything you could wish for in a dessert: White and dark chocolate in one mouthwatering slice.

Serves 10

8 ounces white chocolate, chopped

2½ cups whipping cream

½ cup milk

10 egg yolks

1 tablespoon superfine sugar

scant ½ cup dried coconut

½ cup canned sweetened coconut milk

1¼ cups unsalted macadamia nuts

For the chocolate icing

8 ounces semisweet chocolate

6 tablespoons butter

generous 1 tablespoon light corn syrup

¾ cup whipping cream

curls of fresh coconut, to decorate

1 Line the bottom and sides of a 6-cup terrine mold (10 x 4 inches) with plastic wrap.

2 Place the chopped white chocolate and ½ cup of the cream in the top of a double boiler or in a heatproof bowl set over hot water. Stir until melted and smooth. Set aside.

3 Put 1 cup of the cream and the milk in a pan and bring to the boiling point.

4 Meanwhile, whisk the egg yolks and sugar together in a large bowl until thick and pale.

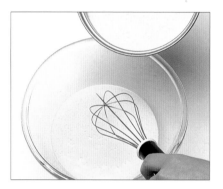

5 Add the hot cream mixture to the yolks, beating constantly. Pour back into the saucepan and cook over low heat for 2–3 minutes, until thickened. Stir constantly and do not boil. Remove the pan from the heat.

6 Add the melted chocolate, dried coconut and coconut milk, then stir well and let cool.

7 Whip the remaining cream until thick, then fold into the chocolate and coconut mixture.

8 Put 2 cups of the parfait mixture in the prepared mold and spread evenly. Cover and freeze for about 2 hours, until just firm. Cover the remaining mixture and chill.

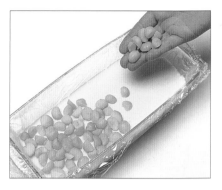

9 Sprinkle the macadamia nuts evenly over the frozen parfait. Pour in the remaining parfait mixture. Cover the terrine and freeze for 6–8 hours or overnight, until the parfait is firm.

10 To make the icing, melt the chocolate with the butter and syrup in the top of a double boiler set over hot water. Stir occasionally.

11 Heat the cream in a saucepan until just simmering, then stir into the chocolate mixture. Remove the pan from the heat and let cool until lukewarm.

12 To turn out the parfait, wrap the terrine in a hot towel and set it upside down on a plate. Lift off the terrine mold, then peel off the plastic wrap. Place the parfait on a rack over a baking sheet and pour the chocolate icing evenly over the top. Working quickly, smooth the icing down the sides with a spatula. Let set slightly, then freeze for another 3–4 hours. Cut into slices using a knife dipped in hot water. Serve, decorated with curls of fresh coconut.

White Chocolate Mousse with Dark Sauce

Creamy vanilla-flavored white chocolate mousse is served with a dark rum and chocolate sauce.

INGREDIENTS

Serves 6–8

7 ounces white chocolate, broken into squares

2 eggs, separated

¼ cup superfine sugar

1¼ cups heavy cream

1 envelope powdered gelatin

⅔ cup plain yogurt

2 teaspoons vanilla extract

For the sauce

2 ounces semisweet chocolate, broken into squares

2 tablespoons dark rum

¼ cup light cream

1 Line a 4-cup loaf pan with waxed paper or plastic wrap. Melt the chocolate in a heatproof bowl over hot water, then remove from the heat.

2 Whisk the egg yolks and sugar in a bowl until pale and thick, then beat in the melted chocolate.

3 Heat the cream in a small saucepan until almost boiling, then remove from the heat. Sprinkle the powdered gelatin over it, stirring gently until it is completely dissolved.

4 Then pour onto the chocolate mixture, whisking vigorously to mix until smooth.

5 Whisk the yogurt and vanilla extract into the mixture. In a clean, grease-free bowl, whisk the egg whites until stiff, then fold them into the mixture. Turn into the prepared loaf pan, level the surface and chill until set.

6 Make the sauce. Melt the chocolate with the rum and cream in a heatproof bowl over barely simmering water, stirring occasionally, then let cool.

7 When the mousse is set, remove it from the pan with the aid of the paper or plastic wrap. Serve in thick slices with the cooled chocolate sauce poured around.

COOK'S TIP

Make sure the gelatin is completely dissolved in the cream before adding to the other ingredients.

Frozen Strawberry Mousse Cake

Children love this pretty dessert – it tastes just like ice cream.

INGREDIENTS

Serves 4–6

1 can (15 ounces) strawberries in syrup

1 envelope powdered gelatin

6 trifle sponge cakes

3 tablespoons strawberry jam

1 cup crème fraîche

1 cup whipped cream, to decorate

1 Strain the syrup from the strawberries into a large heatproof bowl. Sprinkle the gelatin over it and stir well. Stand the bowl in a pan of hot water and stir until the gelatin has dissolved.

2 Let cool, then chill for just under 1 hour, until beginning to set. Meanwhile, cut the sponge cakes in half lengthwise and spread the cut surfaces with the strawberry jam.

3 Carefully whisk the crème fraîche into the strawberry jelly, then whisk in the canned strawberries. Line a deep, 8-inch loose-bottomed cake pan with waxed paper.

4 Pour half the strawberry mousse mixture into the pan, arrange the sponge cakes over the surface, and then spoon over the remaining mousse mixture, pushing down any sponge cakes that rise up.

5 Freeze for 1–2 hours, until firm. Remove the cake from the pan and carefully peel away the lining paper. Transfer to a serving plate. Decorate the mousse with whirls of whipped cream and a few strawberry leaves and a fresh strawberry, if you have them.

Iced Praline Torte

Make this elaborate torte several days ahead, decorate it and return it to the freezer until you are nearly ready to serve it. Let the torte stand at room temperature for an hour before serving, or leave it in the refrigerator overnight to soften.

Serves 8

1 cup almonds or hazelnuts

8 tablespoons superfine sugar

⅔ cup raisins

6 tablespoons rum or brandy

4 ounces dark chocolate, broken into squares

2 tablespoons milk

2 cups heavy cream

2 tablespoons strong black coffee

16 ladyfingers

To finish

⅔ cup heavy cream

½ cup flaked almonds, toasted

½ ounce dark chocolate, melted

1 To make the praline, have ready an oiled cake pan or baking sheet. Put the nuts into a heavy pan with the sugar and heat gently until the sugar melts. Swirl the pan to coat the nuts in the hot sugar. Cook until the nuts brown and the sugar caramelizes. Transfer the nuts quickly to the pan or tray and let them cool completely. Break them up and grind them to a fine powder in a blender or food processor.

2 Soak the raisins in 3 tablespoons of the rum or brandy for an hour (or better still, overnight), so they soften and absorb the rum. Melt the chocolate with the milk in a bowl over a pan of hot, but not boiling, water. Remove and let cool. Lightly grease a 5-cup loaf pan and line it with waxed paper.

3 Whisk the cream in a bowl until it holds soft peaks. Whisk in the cold chocolate. Then fold in the praline and the soaked raisins, with any liquid.

4 Mix the coffee and remaining rum or brandy in a shallow dish. Dip in the ladyfingers and arrange half in a layer over the bottom of the prepared loaf pan.

5 Cover with the chocolate mixture and add another layer of soaked ladyfingers. Leave in the freezer overnight.

6 Whip the heavy cream for the topping. Dip the pan briefly into warm water to loosen it and turn the torte out onto a serving plate. Cover with the whipped cream, sprinkle the top with toasted flaked almonds and drizzle the melted chocolate over the top. Return the torte to the freezer until it is needed.

COOK'S TIP

Make the praline in advance and store it in an airtight jar until needed.

Black Currant Sorbet

Black currants make a vibrant and intensely flavored sorbet.

INGREDIENTS

Serves 4–6

½ cup superfine sugar

1¼ pounds black currants

juice of ½ lemon

1 tablespoon egg white

mint leaves, to decorate

1 In a small saucepan over medium-high heat, bring the sugar and ½ cup of water to a boil, stirring until the sugar dissolves. Boil the syrup for 2 minutes, then remove the pan from the heat and set aside to cool.

2 Remove the black currants from the stalks by pulling them through the tines of a fork.

3 In a blender or food processor fitted with a metal blade, process the black currants and lemon juice until smooth. Alternatively, chop the black currants coarsely, then add the lemon juice. Mix in the sugar syrup.

4 Press the purée through a sieve to remove the seeds.

5 Pour the black currant purée into a non-metallic, freezer-proof dish. Cover the dish with plastic wrap or a lid and freeze until the sorbet is nearly firm, but still a bit slushy.

6 Cut the sorbet into pieces and put into the blender or food processor. Process until smooth, then with the machine running, add the egg white and process until well mixed. Transfer the sorbet back into the dish and freeze until almost firm. Chop the sorbet again and process until smooth.

7 Serve immediately or freeze, tightly covered, for up to 1 week. Let soften for 5–10 minutes at room temperature before serving, decorated with mint leaves.

Chocolate Ice Cream

Use good-quality eating or cooking chocolate for the best flavor.

INGREDIENTS

Makes about 3¾ cups

3 cups milk

1 vanilla bean (4 inches long)

4 egg yolks

¾ cup granulated sugar

8 ounces bittersweet chocolate, melted

1 To make the custard, heat the milk with the vanilla pod in a small saucepan. Remove from the heat as soon as small bubbles start to form. Do not boil.

2 Beat the egg yolks with a wire whisk or electric beater. Gradually incorporate the sugar, and continue beating for about 5 minutes, until the mixture is pale yellow. Strain the milk. Slowly add it to the egg mixture drop by drop.

3 Pour the mixture into a double boiler with the melted chocolate. Stir over medium heat until the water in the pan is boiling and the custard thickens enough to lightly coat the back of a spoon. Remove from the heat and let cool.

4 Freeze in an ice cream maker, or if you do not have an ice cream maker, pour the mixture into a metal or plastic freezer container and freeze until set, about 3 hours. Remove from the container and chop coarsely into 3-inch pieces. Place in the bowl of a food processor and process until smooth. Return to the freezer container, and freeze again until firm. Repeat the freezing-chopping process 2 or 3 times, until a smooth consistency is reached.

Frozen Grand Marnier Soufflés

These sophisticated little soufflés are always appreciated and make a wonderful end to a meal.

INGREDIENTS

Serves 8

1 cup superfine sugar

6 large eggs, separated

1 cup milk

½ ounce powdered gelatin, soaked in
   3 tablespoons cold water

2 cups heavy cream

¼ cup Grand Marnier

1 Tie a double collar of waxed paper around eight ramekins. Put 6 tablespoons of the sugar in a bowl with the egg yolks and whisk until pale.

2 Heat the milk until almost boiling and pour it onto the yolks, whisking all the time. Return to the pan and stir it over gentle heat until it is thick enough to coat the spoon. Remove the pan from the heat and stir in the soaked gelatin. Pour into a bowl and let cool. Whisk occasionally, until it is on the verge of setting.

3 Put the remaining sugar in a pan with 3 tablespoons water and dissolve it over low heat. Bring to a boil and boil rapidly until it reaches the softball stage or 246°F on a sugar thermometer. Remove from the heat. In a clean bowl, whisk the egg whites until they are stiff. Pour the hot syrup onto the whites, whisking constantly. Set aside and let cool.

4 Whisk the cream until it holds soft peaks. Add the Grand Marnier to the cold custard and fold the custard into the cold meringue, with the cream. Quickly pour into the prepared ramekins. Freeze overnight. Remove the paper collars. Let the soufflés stand at room temperature for 30 minutes before serving.

Double Chocolate Snowball

This is an ideal party dessert as it can be prepared at least one day ahead and decorated the day you serve it.

INGREDIENTS

Serves 12–14

12 ounces semisweet chocolate, chopped

1½ cups superfine sugar

1¼ cups unsalted butter, cut into
small pieces

8 eggs

¼ cup orange-flavored liqueur or brandy
(optional)

cocoa for dusting (optional)

For the white chocolate cream

7 ounces fine quality white chocolate,
broken into pieces

2 cups heavy or whipping cream

2 tablespoons orange-flavor liqueur
(optional)

1 Preheat the oven to 350°F. Line a 7½-cup round ovenproof bowl with aluminum foil, smoothing the sides. In a bowl over a pan of simmering water, melt the semisweet chocolate. Add the sugar and stir until it dissolves. Strain into a medium bowl. With an electric mixer at low speed, beat in the butter, then the eggs, one at a time, beating well after each addition. Stir in the liqueur or brandy, if using, and pour into the prepared bowl. Tap gently to release any large air bubbles.

2 Bake for 1¼–1½ hours, until the surface is firm and slightly risen, but cracked. The center will still be wobbly; it will set on cooling. Remove to a rack to cool to room temperature. Cover with a plate, then cover completely with plastic wrap or foil and chill overnight. To unmold, remove the plate and plastic or foil and invert the mold onto a plate; shake firmly to release. Peel off foil. Cover until ready to decorate.

3 Process the white chocolate in a blender or food processor until fine crumbs form. In a small saucepan, heat ½ cup of the cream until just beginning to simmer. With the food processor running, pour the cream through the feed tube and process until the chocolate is completely melted. Strain into a medium bowl and cool to room temperature, stirring occasionally.

4 Beat the remaining cream until soft peaks form, add the liqueur, if using, and beat for 30 seconds or until the cream just holds its shape. Fold a spoonful of cream into the chocolate, then fold in the remaining cream. Spoon into a pastry bag fitted with a star tip and pipe rosettes over the surface. If desired, dust with cocoa.

HOT
DESSERTS

Hot Chocolate Zabaglione

A delicious chocolate-flavored variation of a classic Italian dessert.

INGREDIENTS

Serves 6

6 egg yolks

¾ cup superfine sugar

3 tablespoons cocoa powder

1 cup Marsala

cocoa powder or confectioners' sugar,
   for dusting

almond cookies, to serve

1 Half fill a medium saucepan with water and bring to the simmering point.

2 Place the egg yolks and sugar in a heatproof bowl and whisk until the mixture is pale and all the sugar has dissolved.

3 Add the cocoa and Marsala, then place the bowl over the simmering water. Whisk until the consistency of the mixture is smooth, thick and foamy.

4 Pour quickly into tall heatproof glasses, dust lightly with cocoa or confectioners' sugar and serve immediately with almond cookies.

Chocolate and Orange Scotch Pancakes

Delicious baby pancakes in a rich, creamy orange liqueur sauce.

INGREDIENTS

Serves 4

1 cup self-rising flour

2 tablespoons cocoa powder

2 eggs

2 ounces semisweet chocolate, broken into squares

1 cup milk

finely grated rind of 1 orange

2 tablespoons orange juice

butter or oil for frying

¼ cup chocolate curls, for sprinkling

For the sauce

2 large oranges

2 tablespoons unsalted butter

3 tablespoons light brown sugar

1 cup crème fraîche

2 tablespoons Grand Marnier or Cointreau

1 Sift the flour and cocoa into a bowl and make a well in the center. Add the eggs and beat well, gradually incorporating the surrounding dry ingredients to make a smooth batter.

2 Mix the chocolate and milk in a saucepan. Heat gently until the chocolate has melted, then beat into the batter until smooth and bubbly. Stir in the grated orange rind and juice.

3 Heat a large heavy frying pan or griddle. Grease with a little butter or oil. Drop large spoonfuls of batter onto the hot surface. Cook over medium heat. When the pancakes are lightly browned underneath and bubbly on top, flip them over to cook the other side. Slide onto a plate and keep hot, then make more in the same way.

4 Make the sauce. Grate the rind of 1 of the oranges into a bowl and set aside. Peel both oranges, taking care to remove all the pith, then slice the flesh fairly thinly.

5 Heat the butter and sugar in a wide, shallow pan over low heat, stirring until the sugar dissolves. Stir in the crème fraîche and heat gently.

6 Add the pancakes and orange slices to the sauce, heat gently for 1–2 minutes, then spoon on the liqueur. Sprinkle with the reserved orange rind. Then sprinkle on the chocolate curls and serve the pancakes immediately.

Amaretto Soufflé

A mouthwatering soufflé with more than a hint of Amaretto liqueur.

Serves 6

½ cup superfine sugar

6 amaretti or almond cookies, coarsely crushed

6 tablespoons Amaretto liqueur

4 eggs, separated, plus 1 egg white

2 tablespoons all-purpose flour

1 cup milk

pinch of cream of tartar (if needed)

confectioners' sugar, for dusting

1 Preheat the oven to 400°F. Butter a 6-cup soufflé dish and sprinkle it with a little of the superfine sugar.

2 Put the cookies in a bowl. Sprinkle them with 2 tablespoons of the Amaretto liqueur and set aside.

3 In another bowl, mix together the 4 egg yolks, 2 tablespoons sugar and all the flour.

4 Heat the milk just to a boil in a heavy saucepan. Gradually add the hot milk to the egg mixture, stirring.

5 Pour the mixture back into the pan. Set over low heat and simmer gently for 3–4 minutes or until thickened, stirring occasionally.

6 Add the remaining Amaretto liqueur. Remove from the heat.

7 In a scrupulously clean, grease-free bowl, whisk the 5 egg whites until they hold soft peaks. (If not using a copper bowl, add the cream of tartar as soon as the whites are frothy.) Add the remaining sugar and continue whisking until stiff.

8 Add about one-quarter of the whites to the liqueur mixture and stir in with a rubber spatula. Add the remaining whites and fold in gently.

9 Spoon half the mixture into the prepared soufflé dish. Cover with a layer of the moistened amaretti cookies, then spoon the remaining soufflé mixture on top.

10 Bake for 20 minutes or until the soufflé is risen and lightly browned. Sprinkle with sifted confectioners' sugar and serve immediately.

Hot Mocha Rum Soufflés

Serve these superb soufflés as soon as they are cooked for a fantastic finale to a dinner party.

INGREDIENTS

Serves 6

2 tablespoons unsalted butter, melted

generous ½ cup cocoa powder

generous ⅓ cup superfine sugar

¼ cup strong black coffee

2 tablespoons dark rum

6 egg whites

confectioners' sugar, for dusting

1 Preheat the oven with a baking sheet inside to 375°F. Grease six 1-cup soufflé dishes with the melted butter.

2 Mix 1 tablespoon of the cocoa with 1 tablespoon of the superfine sugar in a bowl. Put the mixture into each of the dishes in turn, rotating them so they are evenly coated.

3 Mix the remaining cocoa with the coffee and rum.

4 Whisk the egg whites in a clean, grease-free bowl until they form firm peaks. Whisk in the remaining superfine sugar. Stir a generous spoonful of the whites into the cocoa mixture to lighten it, then gently fold in the remaining whites.

5 Spoon the mixture into the prepared dishes, smoothing the tops. Place on the hot baking sheet, and bake for 12–15 minutes or until risen. Serve the soufflés immediately, lightly dusted with confectioners' sugar.

COOK'S TIP

When serving the soufflés at the end of a dinner party, prepare them just before the meal is served. Pop in the oven as soon as the main course is finished, and serve freshly baked.

Gingerbread Upside-down Cake

A warm, spicy dessert goes down well on a cold winter's day. This one is quite quick and easy to make and looks very impressive.

INGREDIENTS

Serves 4–6

sunflower oil, for brushing

1 tablespoon brown sugar

4 medium peaches, halved and pitted, or canned peach halves

8 walnut halves

For the cake

generous 1 cup whole-wheat flour

½ teaspoon baking soda

1½ teaspoons ground ginger

1 teaspoon ground cinnamon

½ cup dark brown sugar

1 egg

½ cup skim milk

¼ cup sunflower oil

1 Preheat the oven to 350°F. For the topping, brush the bottom and sides of a 9-inch round springform cake pan with oil. Sprinkle the sugar over the bottom.

2 Arrange the peaches cut-side down in the pan with a walnut half in each.

3 Sift together the flour, baking soda, ginger and cinnamon, then stir in the sugar. Beat the egg, milk and oil, then mix into the dry ingredients.

4 Pour the mixture evenly over the peaches and bake for 35–40 minutes, until firm to the touch. Turn out and serve hot.

Peach Cobbler

A tasty, warm dessert with fresh peaches and almond-flavored pastry.

INGREDIENTS

Serves 6

3 pounds peaches, peeled and sliced

3 tablespoons superfine sugar

2 tablespoons peach brandy

1 tablespoon fresh lemon juice

1 tablespoon cornstarch

For the topping

1 cup all-purpose flour

1½ teaspoons baking powder

¼ teaspoon salt

¼ cup finely ground almonds

¼ cup superfine sugar

¼ cup butter or margarine

½ cup milk

¼ teaspoon almond extract

1 Preheat the oven to 425°F. In a bowl, toss the peaches with the sugar, peach brandy, lemon juice and cornstarch, then spoon the peach mixture into an 8-cup baking dish.

2 For the topping, sift the flour, baking powder and salt into a mixing bowl. Stir in the ground almonds and all but 1 tablespoon of the sugar. With two knives or a pastry blender, cut in the butter or margarine until the mixture resembles coarse bread crumbs.

3 Add the milk and almond extract and stir until the topping mixture is just combined.

4 Drop the topping in spoonfuls onto the peaches. Sprinkle the top with the remaining tablespoon of sugar.

5 Bake until the cobbler topping is browned, 30–35 minutes. Serve hot with ice cream or crème fraîche, if preferred.

Baked Apples with Caramel Sauce

The creamy caramel sauce turns this simple country dessert into a more sophisticated delicacy.

Serves 6

3 Granny Smith apples, cored but not peeled

3 Red Delicious apples, cored but not peeled

¾ cup light brown sugar

½ teaspoon grated nutmeg

¼ teaspoon freshly ground black pepper

¼ cup walnut pieces

scant ¼ cup golden raisins

¼ cup butter or margarine, diced

For the caramel sauce

1 tablespoon butter or margarine

½ cup whipping cream

1 Preheat the oven to 375°F. Grease a baking pan just large enough to hold the apples.

2 With a small knife, cut at an angle to enlarge the core opening at the stem end of each apple to about 1 inch in diameter. (The opening should resemble a funnel in shape.)

3 Arrange the apples in the prepared pan, stem end up.

4 In a small saucepan, combine ¾ cup water with the brown sugar, nutmeg and pepper. Bring the mixture to a boil, stirring. Boil for 6 minutes.

5 Combine the walnuts and raisins. Spoon some of the walnut-raisin mixture into the opening in each apple.

6 Top each apple with some of the diced butter.

7 Spoon the brown sugar sauce over and around the apples. Bake, basting occasionally with the sauce, until the apples are just tender, 45–50 minutes. Transfer the apples to a serving dish, reserving the brown sugar sauce in the baking pan. Keep the apples warm.

8 For the caramel sauce, mix the butter, cream and reserved brown sugar sauce in a saucepan. Bring to a boil, stirring occasionally, and simmer until thickened, about 2 minutes. Let the sauce cool slightly before serving.

VARIATION

Use a mixture of firm red and gold pears instead of the apples, preparing them in the same way. Cook for 10 minutes longer.

Baked Apples with Apricot Filling

An alternative stuffing mixture for baked apples with a refreshing fruit flavor.

Serves 6

scant ½ cup chopped dried apricots

½ cup chopped walnuts

1 teaspoon grated lemon rind

½ teaspoon ground cinnamon

½ cup light brown sugar

2 tablespoons butter, at room temperature

6 large eating apples

1 tablespoon melted butter

1 Preheat the oven to 375°F. Place the apricots, walnuts, lemon rind and cinnamon in a bowl. Add the sugar and butter and stir until thoroughly mixed.

2 Core the apples, without cutting all the way through to the base. Peel the top of each apple and then slightly widen the top of each opening to make room for the filling.

3 Spoon the filling into the apples, packing it down lightly.

4 Place the stuffed apples in an ovenproof dish large enough to hold them all comfortably side by side.

5 Brush the apples with the melted butter. Bake for 45–50 minutes, until they are tender. Serve hot.

COOK'S TIP

Accompany with real custard (Crème Anglaise), made using cream, egg yolks, superfine sugar and a few drops of vanilla extract.

Pears in Chocolate Fudge Blankets

Warm poached pears coated in a rich chocolate fudge sauce – who could resist?

Serves 6

6 ripe eating pears
2 tablespoons lemon juice
scant ½ cup superfine sugar
1 cinnamon stick

For the sauce
1 cup heavy cream
scant 1 cup light brown sugar
2 tablespoons unsalted butter
¼ cup light corn syrup
½ cup milk
7 ounces semisweet dark chocolate,
    broken into squares

1 Peel the pears, leaving the stalks on. Scoop out the cores from the base. Brush the cut surfaces with lemon juice to prevent browning.

2 Place the sugar and 1¼ cups water in a large saucepan. Heat gently until the sugar dissolves. Add the pears and cinnamon stick with any remaining lemon juice, and, if necessary, a little more water, so the pears are almost covered.

3 Bring to a boil, then lower the heat, cover the pan and simmer the pears gently for 15-20 minutes.

4 Meanwhile, make the sauce. Place the cream, sugar, butter, corn syrup and milk in a heavy saucepan. Heat gently until the sugar has dissolved and the butter and syrup have melted, then bring to a boil. Boil, stirring constantly, for about 5 minutes or until thick and smooth.

5 Remove the pan from the heat and stir in the chocolate, stirring until it has all melted.

6 Using a slotted spoon, transfer the poached pears to a dish. Keep hot. Boil the syrup rapidly to reduce it to about 3–4 tablespoons. Remove the cinnamon stick and gently stir the syrup into the chocolate sauce.

7 Serve the pears in individual bowls or on dessert plates, with the hot chocolate fudge sauce spooned over them.

Steamed Walnut Toffee Pudding

Filling, warming and packed with calories, but still everyone's favorite pudding.

INGREDIENTS

Serves 6

1 cup toasted walnuts, chopped

¾ cup butter

scant 1 cup brown sugar

¼ cup light cream

2 tablespoons lemon juice

2 eggs, beaten

1 cup self-rising flour

1 Grease a 4-cup pudding mold and add half the walnuts.

2 Heat ¼ cup of the butter with ¼ cup of the sugar, the cream and 1 tablespoon lemon juice in a small pan, stirring until smooth. Pour half into the pudding mold, then swirl to coat it a little way up the sides.

3 Beat the remaining butter and sugar until light and fluffy, then gradually beat in the eggs. Fold in the flour and the remaining nuts and lemon juice and spoon into the mold .

4 Cover the mold with waxed paper with a pleat folded in the center, then tie securely with string.

5 Steam the pudding for about 1¼ hours, until it is set in the center.

6 Just before serving, gently warm the remaining sauce. Unmold the pudding onto a warm plate and pour the warm sauce over it.

Chocolate and Orange Soufflé

The base in this soufflé is an easy-to-make semolina mixture, rather than the thick white sauce that most soufflés call for.

INGREDIENTS

Serves 4

2½ cups milk

generous ⅓ cup semolina

scant ¼ cup brown sugar

grated rind of 1 orange

6 tablespoons fresh orange juice

3 eggs, separated

3 ounces semisweet chocolate, grated

confectioners' sugar, for sprinkling

1 Preheat the oven to 400°F. Butter a shallow 8-cup ovenproof dish, and set it aside while you prepare the soufflé.

2 Pour the milk into a heavy saucepan, sprinkle in the semolina and brown sugar, then heat, stirring the mixture constantly, until boiling and thickened.

3 Remove the pan from the heat, beat in the orange rind and juice, egg yolks and all but 1 tablespoon of the grated chocolate.

4 Whisk the egg whites until stiff, then lightly fold into the semolina mixture in three batches. Spoon into the buttered dish and bake for about 30 minutes, until just set in the center. Sprinkle with the reserved chocolate and the confectioners' sugar.

Queen of Desserts

This English pudding was developed from a seventeenth-century recipe by Queen Victoria's chefs and named in her honor.

INGREDIENTS

Serves 4

1½ cups fresh bread crumbs

¼ cup superfine sugar, plus
   1 teaspoon

grated lemon rind

2½ cups milk

4 eggs

3 tablespoons raspberry jam, warmed

1 Preheat the oven to 325°F. Stir the bread crumbs, 2 tablespoons of the sugar and the lemon rind together in a bowl. Bring the milk to a boil in a saucepan, then stir into the bread crumb mixture.

2 Separate three of the eggs and beat the yolks with the whole egg. Stir into the bread crumb mixture, pour into a buttered baking dish and let stand for 30 minutes, then bake the pudding for 50–60 minutes, until set.

COOK'S TIP
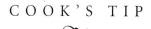

For tasty changes, use another flavored jam, lemon curd, marmalade or fruit purée.

3 Whisk the three egg whites in a large, clean bowl until stiff, but not dry, then gradually whisk in the remaining 2 tablespoons superfine sugar until the mixture is thick and glossy, taking care not to overwhip.

4 Spread the jam over the pudding, then spoon on the meringue to cover the top completely. Sprinkle the remaining sugar over the meringue, then bake for another 15 minutes, until the meringue is beginning to turn a light golden color.

Apple Couscous Pudding

*This unusual couscous mixture
makes a delicious family dessert
with a rich fruit flavor, but
virtually no fat.*

Serves 4

2½ cups apple juice

⅔ cup couscous

scant ¼ cup golden raisins

½ teaspoon pumpkin pie spice

1 large Cortland apple, peeled,
  cored and sliced

2 tablespoons raw sugar

plain low-fat yogurt, to serve

1 Preheat the oven to 400°F.
Place the apple juice, couscous,
raisins and spice in a pan and
bring to a boil, stirring. Cover and
simmer for 10–12 minutes, until
all the liquid is absorbed.

COOK'S TIP

For easy changes, substitute
other dried fruits for the raisins
in this recipe – try chopped dates
or pears, figs or apricots.

2 Spoon half the couscous
mixture into a 5-cup
ovenproof dish and top with half
the apple slices. Top with the
remaining couscous.

3 Arrange the remaining apple
slices to overlap on the top
and sprinkle with raw sugar. Bake
for 25–30 minutes, or until the
apples are golden brown. Serve
hot with yogurt.

Cabinet Pudding

A rich, baked custard, flavored with candied and dried fruit.

INGREDIENTS

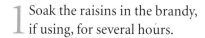

Serves 4

3 tablespoons raisins, chopped

2 tablespoons brandy (optional)

3 tablespoons candied cherries, halved

3 tablespoons angelica, chopped

2 trifle sponge cakes, diced

2 ounces macaroons, crushed

2 eggs

2 egg yolks

2 tablespoons sugar

2 cups light cream or milk

few drops vanilla extract

1 Soak the raisins in the brandy, if using, for several hours.

2 Butter a 3-cup charlotte mold and arrange some of the cherries and angelica in the base.

3 Mix the remaining cherries and angelica with the sponge cakes, macaroons and raisins, and spoon into the mold.

4 Lightly whisk together the eggs, egg yolks and sugar. Bring the cream just to a boil, then stir into the egg mixture with the vanilla extract.

5 Strain the egg mixture into the mold, then let stand for 15–30 minutes.

6 Preheat the oven to 325°F. Place the mold in a roasting pan, cover with waxed paper and pour in boiling water to come halfway up the side of the mold. Bake for 1 hour, or until set. Let stand for 2–3 minutes, then turn out onto a warm plate, to serve.

Eve's Cake

The tempting apples beneath the sponge topping are the reason for the cake's name.

INGREDIENTS

Serves 4–6

½ cup butter

generous ½ cup superfine sugar

2 eggs, beaten

grated rind and juice of 1 lemon

scant 1 cup self-rising flour

⅓ cup ground almonds

scant ½ cup brown sugar

1½ pounds cooking apples, cored and thinly sliced

¼ cup flaked almonds

1 Beat together the butter and superfine sugar in a large mixing bowl until the mixture is very light and fluffy.

2 Gradually beat the eggs into the butter mixture, beating well after each addition, then fold in the lemon rind, flour and ground almonds.

3 Mix the brown sugar, apples and lemon juice, turn into the dish, add the cake batter, then the almonds. Bake for 40–45 minutes, until golden.

Chocolate Crêpes with Plums and Port

A good dinner party dessert, this dish can be made in advance and always looks impressive.

INGREDIENTS

Serves 6

2 ounces semisweet chocolate, broken into
    squares
1 cup milk
½ cup light cream, or half-and-half
2 tablespoons cocoa powder
1 cup all-purpose flour
2 eggs

For the filling

1¼ pounds red or golden plums
¼ cup superfine sugar
2 tablespoons port
oil, for frying
¾ cup crème fraîche

For the sauce

5 ounces semisweet chocolate, broken into
    squares
¾ cup heavy cream
2 tablespoons port

1 Place the chocolate in a saucepan with the milk. Heat gently until the chocolate has dissolved. Pour into a blender or food processor and add the cream, cocoa powder, flour and eggs. Process until smooth, then pour into a bowl and chill for 30 minutes.

2 Meanwhile, make the filling. Halve and pit the plums. Place them in a saucepan and add the sugar and 2 tablespoons water. Bring to a boil, then lower the heat, cover, and simmer for about 10 minutes or until the plums are tender. Stir in the port; simmer for another 30 seconds. Remove the pan from the heat and keep warm.

3 Have ready a sheet of waxed paper. Heat a crêpe pan, grease it lightly with a little oil, then pour in just enough batter to cover the bottom of the pan, swirling to coat it evenly.

4 Cook until the crêpe has set, then flip it over to cook the other side. Slide the crêpe out onto the sheet of paper, then cook 9–11 more crêpes in the same way.

5 Make the sauce. Combine the chocolate and cream in a saucepan. Heat gently, stirring until smooth. Add the port and heat gently, stirring, for 1 minute.

6 Divide the plum filling between the crêpes, add a dollop of crème fraîche to each and roll them up carefully. Serve in shallow plates, with the chocolate sauce spooned over the top.

Chocolate Soufflé Crêpes

*A nonstick pan is ideal as it does not
need greasing between each crêpe.
Serve two crêpes per person.*

Makes 12 crêpes

⅔ cup all-purpose flour

1 tablespoon unsweetened cocoa

1 teaspoon superfine sugar

pinch of salt

1 teaspoon ground cinnamon

2 eggs

¾ cup milk

1 teaspoon vanilla extract

¼ cup unsalted butter, melted

confectioners' sugar, for dusting

raspberries, pineapple and mint sprigs,
   to decorate

For the pineapple syrup

½ medium pineapple, peeled, cored and
   finely chopped

2 tablespoons pure maple syrup

1 teaspoon cornstarch

½ cinnamon stick

2 tablespoons rum

For the soufflé filling

9 ounces semisweet or bittersweet
   chocolate

⅓ cup heavy cream

3 eggs, separated

2 tablespoons superfine sugar

1 Prepare syrup. In a saucepan over medium heat, bring the pineapple, ½ cup water, maple syrup, cornstarch and cinnamon stick to a boil. Simmer for 2–3 minutes, until the sauce thickens, whisking frequently. Remove from heat; discard the cinnamon stick. Pour into a bowl, stir in rum and chill.

2 Prepare crêpes. In a bowl, sift the flour, cocoa, sugar, salt and cinnamon. Stir to blend, then make a well in the center. In a bowl, beat the eggs, milk and vanilla and gradually add to the well, whisking in flour from the side to form a smooth batter. Stir in half the melted butter and pour batter into a bowl. Let stand for 1 hour.

3 Heat a 7–8-inch crêpe pan. Brush with butter. Stir the batter. Pour 3 tablespoons batter into the pan; swirl pan quickly to cover bottom with a thin layer. Cook over medium-high heat for 1–2 minutes, until bottom is golden. Turn over and cook for 30–45 seconds, then turn onto a plate. Stack crêpes between non-stick waxed paper and set aside.

4 Prepare filling. In a small saucepan, over medium heat, melt the chocolate and cream until smooth, stirring frequently.

5 In a bowl, beat the yolks with half the sugar for 3–5 minutes, until light and creamy. Gradually beat in the chocolate mixture. Let cool. In a large bowl, beat the egg whites until soft peaks form. Gradually beat in the remaining sugar until stiff. Beat a spoonful of egg whites into the chocolate mixture, then fold in the remaining whites.

6 Preheat the oven to 400°F. Lay a crêpe on a plate. Spoon a little soufflé mixture on the crêpe, spreading it to the edge. Fold the bottom half over the soufflé mixture, then fold in half again to form a filled "triangle." Place on a buttered baking sheet. Repeat with the remaining crêpes.

7 Brush the tops with butter and bake for 15–20 minutes, until the filling has souffléd. Dust with confectioners' sugar and garnish with raspberries, pineapple, mint and pineapple syrup.

Warm Lemon and Syrup Cake

The combination of pears, syrup and lemon makes this a real winner. Drizzle with light cream for extra luxury.

INGREDIENTS

Serves 8

3 eggs

¾ cup butter, softened

¾ cup superfine sugar

1½ cups self-rising flour

½ cup ground almonds

¼ teaspoon freshly grated nutmeg

5 tablespoons candied lemon peel, finely chopped

grated rind of 1 lemon

2 tablespoons lemon juice

poached pears, to serve

For the syrup

¾ cup superfine sugar

juice of 3 lemons

1 Preheat the oven to 350°F. Grease and line the bottom of a deep, round 8-inch cake pan with waxed paper.

2 Place all the cake ingredients in a large bowl and beat well for 2–3 minutes, until the mixture is light and fluffy.

3 Turn the mixture into the prepared pan, spread level and bake for 1 hour or until golden and firm to the touch.

4 Meanwhile, make the syrup. Put the sugar, lemon juice and 5 tablespoons water in a pan. Heat gently, stirring until the sugar has dissolved, then boil, without stirring, for 1–2 minutes.

5 Turn out the cake onto a plate with a rim. Prick the surface of the cake all over with a fork, then pour the hot syrup over it. Let soak for about 30 minutes. Serve the cake warm with thin wedges of poached pears.

Magic Chocolate Mud Cake

A popular favorite, which magically separates into a light and luscious sponge and a velvety chocolate sauce.

INGREDIENTS

Serves 4

¼ cup butter

generous 1 cup light brown sugar

2 cups milk

scant 1 cup self-rising flour

1 teaspoon ground cinnamon

5 tablespoons cocoa powder

plain yogurt or vanilla ice cream, to serve

1 Preheat the oven to 350°F. Lightly grease a 6-cup, straight-sided ovenproof dish and place on a baking sheet.

2 Place the butter in a saucepan. Add ¾ cup of the sugar and ⅔ cup of the milk. Heat gently, stirring occasionally, until the butter has melted and all the sugar has dissolved. Remove the pan from the heat.

3 Sift the flour, cinnamon and 1 tablespoon of the cocoa powder into the pan and stir into the mixture, mixing evenly. Pour the mixture into the prepared dish and level the surface.

4 Sift the remaining sugar and cocoa powder into a bowl, mix well, then sprinkle it over the cake mixture.

5 Pour the remaining milk over the cake.

6 Bake for 45–50 minutes or until the sponge has risen to the top and is firm to the touch. Serve hot, with yogurt or vanilla ice cream.

COOK'S TIP

A soufflé dish will support the sponge as it rises above the sauce.

Christmas Steamed Pudding

This recipe makes enough to fill one 5-cup mold or two 2½-cup molds. It can be made up to a month before Christmas and stored in a cool, dry place. Steam the pudding for 2 hours before serving. Serve with brandy or rum butter, whiskey sauce, custard or whipped cream, topped with a decorative sprig of holly.

INGREDIENTS

Serves 8

½ cup butter

1 rounded cup dark brown sugar

½ cup self-rising flour

1 teaspoon ground pumpkin pie spice

¼ teaspoon grated nutmeg

½ teaspoon ground cinnamon

2 eggs

2 cups fresh white bread crumbs

generous 1 cup golden raisins

generous 1 cup dark raisins

½ cup currants

3 tablespoons mixed candied peel, chopped finely

¼ cup chopped almonds

1 small cooking apple, peeled, cored and coarsely grated

finely grated rind of 1 orange or lemon

juice of 1 orange or lemon, made up to ⅔ cup with brandy, rum or sherry

1 Cut a circle of waxed paper to fit the bottom of the mold(s) and butter the disc and mold(s).

2 Whisk the butter and sugar together until soft. Beat in the flour, spices and eggs. Stir in the remaining ingredients thoroughly. The mixture should have a soft dropping consistency.

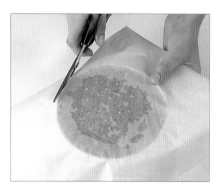

3 Turn the mixture into the greased mold(s) and level the top with a spoon.

4 Cover with another circle of buttered waxed paper.

5 Make two pleats across the center of a large piece of waxed paper and cover the mold(s) with it, tying it in place with string under the rim. Cut off the excess paper. Pleat a piece of foil in the same way and cover the mold(s) with it, tucking it around the bowl neatly, under the wax frill. Tie another piece of string around and across the top, as a handle.

6 Place the mold(s) in a steamer over a pan of simmering water and steam for 6 hours. Alternatively, put the mold(s) into a large pan and pour around enough boiling water to come halfway up the mold(s) and cover the pan with a tight-fitting lid. Check that the water is simmering and add boiling water as it evaporates. When the mold(s) have cooked, let cool completely. Then remove the foil and waxed paper. Wipe the mold(s) clean and replace the waxed paper and foil with clean pieces, ready for reheating.

TO SERVE

Steam for 2 hours. Turn onto a plate, and let stand for 5 minutes before removing the pudding mold (the steam will rise to the top of the basin and help loosen the pudding). Decorate with a sprig of holly.

Steamed Chocolate and Fruit Desserts

Some things always turn out well, including these wonderful little desserts. Dark, fluffy chocolate sponge with tangy cranberries and apple is served with a honeyed chocolate syrup.

INGREDIENTS

Serves 4

⅔ cup dark brown sugar

1 eating apple

¾ cup cranberries, thawed if frozen

½ cup soft margarine

2 eggs

⅔ cup all-purpose flour

½ teaspoon baking powder

3 tablespoons cocoa powder

For the chocolate syrup

4 ounces semisweet chocolate, broken into squares

2 tablespoons clear honey

1 tablespoon unsalted butter

½ teaspoon vanilla extract

1 Prepare a steamer or half fill a saucepan with water and bring it to a boil. Grease four individual pudding molds and sprinkle each one with a little of the brown sugar to coat well all over.

2 Peel and core the apple. Dice it into a bowl, add the cranberries and mix well. Divide equally among the prepared pudding basins.

3 Place the remaining brown sugar in a mixing bowl. Add the margarine, eggs, flour, baking powder and cocoa; beat until combined and smooth.

4 Spoon the mixture into the basins and cover each with a double thickness of foil. Steam for about 45 minutes, adding boiling water as required, until the desserts are risen and firm.

5 Make the syrup. Mix the chocolate, honey, butter and vanilla extract in a small saucepan. Heat gently, stirring, until melted and smooth.

6 Run a knife around the edge of each pudding to loosen it, then turn out onto individual plates. Serve immediately, with the chocolate syrup.

COOK'S TIP

The desserts can be cooked very quickly in the microwave. Use nonmetallic molds and cover with waxed paper instead of foil. Cook on High (100% power) for 5–6 minutes, then stand for 2–3 minutes before turning out.

Hot Chocolate Cake

*This is wonderfully wicked served
as a dessert with a white chocolate
sauce. The basic cake freezes well –
thaw, then warm in the microwave
before serving.*

INGREDIENTS

Makes 10–12 slices

1¾ cups self-rising whole-wheat flour

¼ cup cocoa powder

pinch of salt

¾ cup soft margarine

¾ cup light brown sugar

few drops vanilla extract

4 eggs

3 ounces white chocolate, coarsely chopped

chocolate leaves and curls, to decorate

For the white chocolate sauce

3 ounces white chocolate

⅔ cup light cream or half-and-half

2–3 tablespoons milk

1 Preheat the oven to 325°F. Sift
the flour, cocoa powder and
salt into a bowl, adding in the
whole-wheat flakes from the sieve.

2 Cream the margarine, sugar
and vanilla extract together
until light and fluffy, then gently
beat in one egg.

3 Gradually stir in the remaining
eggs, one at a time, alternately
folding in some of the flour, until
the mixture is blended in.

4 Stir in the white chocolate and
spoon into a 1½–2 pound loaf
pan or a 7-inch greased cake pan.
Bake for 30–40 minutes, or until
just firm to the touch and
shrinking away from the sides of
the pan.

5 Meanwhile, prepare the sauce.
Heat the white chocolate and
cream very gently in a pan until
the chocolate is melted. Add the
milk and stir until cool.

6 Serve the cake sliced, in a pool
of sauce and decorated with
chocolate leaves and curls.

Chocolate Almond Meringue Pie

This dream dessert combines three very popular flavors: velvety chocolate filling on a light orange pastry case, topped with fluffy meringue.

INGREDIENTS

Serves 6

1½ cups all-purpose flour

⅓ cup ground rice

⅔ cup unsalted butter

finely grated rind of 1 orange

1 egg yolk

flaked almonds and melted plain dark
    chocolate, to decorate

For the filling

5 ounces semisweet dark chocolate,
    broken into squares

¼ cup unsalted butter, softened

⅓ cup superfine sugar

2 teaspoons cornstarch

4 egg yolks

¾ cup ground almonds

For the meringue

3 egg whites

¾ cup superfine sugar

1 Sift the flour and ground rice into a bowl. Rub in the butter until the mixture resembles bread crumbs. Stir in the orange rind. Add the egg yolk; bring the dough together. Roll out and use to line a 9-inch round tart pan. Chill for 30 minutes.

2 Preheat the oven to 375°F. Prick the pastry shell all over with a fork, cover with waxed paper weighed down with baking beans and bake blind for 10 minutes. Remove the pastry shell; take out the baking beans and paper.

3 Make the filling. Melt the chocolate in a heatproof bowl over hot water. Cream the butter with the sugar in a bowl, then beat in the cornstarch and egg yolks. Fold in the almonds, then the chocolate. Spread in the pastry shell. Bake for another 10 minutes.

4 Make the meringue. Whisk the egg whites until stiff, then gradually add half the superfine sugar. Fold in remaining sugar.

5 Spoon the meringue over the chocolate filling, lifting it up with the back of the spoon to form peaks. Reduce the oven temperature to 350°F, and bake the pie for 15–20 minutes, or until the topping is pale gold. Serve warm, scattered with almonds and drizzled with melted chocolate.

Chocolate Chip and Banana Pudding

Hot and steamy, this superb light pudding tastes extra special served with chocolate sauce.

INGREDIENTS

Serves 4

1¾ cups self-rising flour

6 tablespoons unsalted butter or margarine

2 ripe bananas

⅓ cup superfine sugar

¼ cup milk

1 egg, beaten

¼ cup semisweet chocolate chips or chopped chocolate

Glossy Chocolate Sauce and whipped cream, to serve

1 Prepare a steamer or half fill a saucepan with water and bring it to a boil. Grease a 4-cup pudding mold. Sift the flour into a bowl and rub in the butter until the mixture resembles bread crumbs.

2 Mash the bananas in a bowl. Stir them into the creamed mixture, with the sugar.

3 Whisk the milk with the egg in a cup or bowl, then beat into the pudding mixture. Stir in the chocolate chips or chopped chocolate.

4 Spoon the mixture into the prepared mold, cover closely with a double thickness of foil, and steam for 2 hours, replacing the water as required during cooking.

5 Run a knife around the top of the pudding to loosen it, then turn it out onto a warm serving dish. Serve hot, with the chocolate sauce and a spoonful of whipped cream.

COOK'S TIP

If you have a food processor, make a quick-mix version by processing all the ingredients, except the chocolate, until smooth. Stir in the chocolate and proceed as in the recipe.

Hot Plum Batter Cake

Other fruits can be used instead of plums, depending on the season. Canned dark cherries are a convenient substitute to keep in the pantry.

INGREDIENTS

Serves 4

1 pound ripe red plums, quartered and
    pitted

1 cup skim milk

¼ cup skim milk powder

1 tablespoon light brown sugar

1 teaspoon vanilla extract

⅔ cup self-rising flour

2 egg whites

confectioners' sugar, to sprinkle

1 Preheat the oven to 425°F.
Lightly oil a wide, shallow ovenproof dish and add the plums.

2 Pour the milk, milk powder, sugar, vanilla, flour and egg whites into a blender or food processor. Process until smooth.

3 Pour the batter over the plums. Bake for 25–30 minutes, or until puffed and golden. Sprinkle with confectioners' sugar and serve immediately.

COOK'S TIP

If you don't have a food processor, then place the dry ingredients for the batter in a large bowl and gradually whisk in the milk and egg whites.

Glazed Apricot Sponge Cake

Many desserts can be very high in saturated fat, but this healthy version uses the minimum of oil and no eggs.

INGREDIENTS

Serves 4

2 teaspoons light corn syrup

1 can (15 ounces) apricot halves in fruit
    juice

1¼ cups self-rising flour

1½ cups fresh bread crumbs

½ cup light brown sugar

1 teaspoon ground cinnamon

2 tablespoons sunflower oil

¾ cup skim milk

1 Preheat the oven to 350°F.
Lightly oil a 4-cup pudding mold. Spoon in the syrup.

2 Drain the apricots and reserve the juice. Arrange about 8 halves in the mold. Purée the rest of the apricots with the juice and set aside.

3 Mix the flour, bread crumbs, sugar and cinnamon, then beat in the oil and milk. Spoon into the mold and bake for 50–55 minutes, or until firm and golden. Turn out and serve with the puréed fruit as an accompaniment.

QUICK AND EASY

Frudités with Honey Dip

A colorful and tasty variation on the popular savory crudités.

Serves 4

1 cup plain yogurt

3 tablespoons honey

selection of fresh fruit for dipping, such as apples, pears, tangerines, grapes, figs, cherries, strawberries and kiwi fruit

1 Place the yogurt in a dish, beat until smooth, then partially stir in the honey, leaving a marbled effect.

2 Cut the various fruits into wedges or bite-sized pieces or leave whole.

3 Arrange the fruits on a platter with the bowl of dip in the center. Serve chilled.

COOK'S TIP

Sprinkle the apple and pear wedges with lemon juice to prevent discoloring.

Watermelon, Ginger and Grapefruit Salad

This pretty, pink combination is very light and refreshing for any summer meal.

Serves 4

2 cups diced watermelon

2 ruby or pink grapefruit

2 pieces preserved ginger in syrup

2 tablespoons preserved ginger syrup

whipped cream, to serve

1 Remove any seeds from the watermelon and cut into bite-sized chunks.

2 Using a small, sharp knife, cut away all the peel and white pith from the grapefruit and carefully lift out the segments, catching any juice in a bowl.

COOK'S TIP

Toss the fruits gently – grapefruit segments will break up easily and the appearance of the dish will be spoiled.

3 Finely chop the preserved ginger and place in a serving bowl with the melon cubes and grapefruit segments, adding the reserved juice.

4 Spoon on the ginger syrup and toss the fruits lightly to mix evenly. Chill before serving with a bowl of whipped cream.

Yogurt with Apricots and Pistachios

If you let plain yogurt drain overnight, it becomes much thicker and more luscious. Add honeyed apricots and nuts and you have an exotic, yet simple, dessert.

INGREDIENTS

Serves 4

1 pound plain yogurt

⅔ cup dried apricots, chopped

1 tablespoon honey

orange rind, grated

2 tablespoons unsalted pistachios, chopped

ground cinnamon

1 Place the yogurt in a fine sieve and let it drain overnight in the fridge over a bowl.

2 Discard the whey from the yogurt. Place the apricots in a saucepan, barely cover with water and simmer for just 3 minutes, to soften. Drain and cool, then mix with the honey.

3 Mix the yogurt with the apricots, orange rind and nuts. Spoon into sundae dishes, sprinkle on a little cinnamon and chill.

VARIATION

For a simple dessert, strain the fruit, cover with yogurt and sprinkle with raw sugar and a little mixed spice or cinnamon.

Fresh Pineapple Salad

This very refreshing salad can be prepared ahead. Orange flower water is available at Middle Eastern food stores or good delicatessens.

INGREDIENTS

Serves 4

1 small ripe pineapple

confectioners' sugar, to taste

1 tablespoon orange flower water, or more if desired

good ½ cup fresh dates, pitted and quartered

8 ounces fresh strawberries, sliced

fresh mint sprigs, to decorate

1 Cut the skin from the pineapple, and using the tip of a vegetable peeler, remove as many brown "eyes" as possible. Quarter lengthwise, remove the core, then slice.

2 Lay the pineapple in a shallow glass bowl. Sprinkle with sugar and orange flower water.

3 Add the dates and strawberries to the pineapple, cover and chill for at least 2 hours, stirring once or twice. Serve lightly chilled, decorated with a few mint sprigs.

Figs with Ricotta Cream

Fresh, ripe figs are full of natural sweetness and need little adornment. This simple recipe makes the most of their beautiful, intense flavor.

INGREDIENTS

Serves 4

4 ripe fresh figs

½ cup ricotta or cottage cheese

3 tablespoons crème fraîche

1 tablespoon honey

½ teaspoon vanilla extract

freshly grated nutmeg, to decorate

3 Combine the ricotta cheese, crème fraîche, honey and vanilla.

1 Trim the stalks from the figs. Make four cuts through each fig at the stalk end, cutting them almost through but leaving them joined at the base.

2 Place the figs on serving plates and open them out.

4 Spoon a little ricotta cream on each plate and sprinkle with grated nutmeg to serve.

Three-fruits Compote

Mixing dried fruits with fresh ones makes a good combination, especially if flavored delicately with a little orange flower water. A melon ball scoop gives the compote a classy touch, but you could chop the melon into cubes.

Serves 6

¾ cup dried apricots

1 small ripe pineapple

1 small ripe melon

1 tablespoon orange flower water

fresh mint sprig, to decorate

1 Put the apricots into a saucepan with 1¼ cups water. Bring to a boil, then simmer for 5 minutes. Set aside to cool.

2 Peel and quarter the pineapple, then cut the core from each quarter and discard. Cut the flesh into chunks.

3 Seed the melon and scoop balls from the flesh. Save any juices that fall from the fruits and add them to the apricots.

4 Stir in the orange flower water and combine all the fruits. Pour into a serving dish, decorate with mint and chill.

VARIATION

A good fruit salad doesn't need to be a boring mixture of multi-colored fruits swimming in sweet syrup. Instead of the usual apple, orange and grape salad, give it a theme, such as red berry fruits, or a variety of sliced green fruits – even a dish of just one fruit nicely prepared and sprinkled lightly with some sugar and fresh lemon juice can look beautiful and tastes delicious. Do not use more than three fruits in a salad so the flavors remain distinct.

Prune and Orange Pots

A simple pantry dessert, made in minutes. It can be served immediately, but it's best chilled for about half an hour before serving.

Serves 4

1 cup dried prunes

⅔ cup orange juice

1 cup low-fat plain yogurt

shreds of orange rind, to decorate

1 Remove the pits from the prunes and coarsely chop them. Place them in a pan with the orange juice.

2 Bring the juice to a boil, stirring. Reduce the heat, cover and let simmer for 5 minutes, until the prunes are tender and the liquid is reduced by half.

3 Remove from the heat, let cool slightly and then beat well with a wooden spoon, until the fruit breaks down to a coarse purée.

4 Transfer the mixture to a bowl. Stir in the yogurt, swirling the yogurt and fruit purée together lightly, to give an attractive marbled effect.

5 Spoon the mixture into stemmed glasses or individual dishes, smoothing the tops.

6 Top each dish with a few shreds of orange rind, to decorate. Chill before serving.

VARIATION

This dessert can also be made with other dried fruits, such as apricots or peaches. For a special occasion, add a dash of brandy or Cointreau with the yogurt.

Quick Apricot Blender Whip

One of the quickest desserts you could make – as well as one of the prettiest.

INGREDIENTS

Serves 4

1 can (14 ounces) apricot halves in juice

1 tablespoon Grand Marnier or brandy

¾ cup plain yogurt

2 tablespoons sliced almonds

1 Drain the juice from the apricots and place the fruit and liqueur in a blender or food processor.

2 Process the apricots to a smooth purée.

3 Spoon the fruit purée and yogurt in alternate spoonfuls into four tall glasses or glass dishes, swirling them together gently to give a marbled effect.

4 Lightly toast the almonds until they are golden. Let them cool slightly and then sprinkle them over the top.

COOK'S TIP

For an even lighter dessert, use low-fat instead of whole-fat yogurt and a little fruit juice from the can instead of liqueur.

Emerald Fruit Salad

This mixture of green and golden fruit both looks and tastes refreshing.

INGREDIENTS

Serves 4

2 tablespoons lime juice

2 tablespoons honey

2 green eating apples, cored and sliced

1 small ripe cantaloupe, diced

2 kiwi fruit, sliced

1 star fruit, sliced

fresh mint sprigs, to decorate

yogurt or fromage frais, to serve

1 Mix together the lime juice and honey in a large bowl, then toss in the apple slices.

2 Carefully stir in the cantaloupe, kiwi fruit and star fruit. Place in a glass serving dish and chill before serving.

3 Decorate with mint sprigs and serve with yogurt or fromage frais.

COOK'S TIP

Star fruit is best when fully ripe – look for plump, yellow fruit.

Peach and Ginger Paskha

This simple adaptation of a Russian Easter favorite is made with much lighter ingredients than the traditional version.

INGREDIENTS

Serves 4–6

1½ cups low-fat cottage cheese

2 ripe peaches or nectarines

scant ⅓ cup low-fat plain yogurt

2 pieces preserved ginger in syrup, drained and chopped

2 tablespoons preserved ginger syrup

½ teaspoon vanilla extract

peach slices and toasted sliced almonds, to decorate

1 Drain the cottage cheese and press through a sieve into a bowl. Pit and coarsely chop the peaches.

2 Combine the chopped peaches, cottage cheese, yogurt, ginger, syrup and vanilla extract.

3 Line a new, clean flowerpot or a sieve with a piece of clean, fine cloth such as muslin.

4 Put in the cheese mixture, then wrap the cloth over it and place a weight on top. Set over a bowl and let sit in a cool place to drain overnight. To serve, unwrap the cloth and invert the paskha onto a plate. Decorate with peach slices and almonds.

Raspberry and Passion Fruit Swirls

If passion fruit is not available, this simple dessert can be made with raspberries alone.

INGREDIENTS

Serves 4

scant 2 cups raspberries

2 passion fruit

1⅔ cups low-fat cream cheese

2 tablespoons granulated sugar

raspberries and fresh mint sprigs, to decorate

1 Mash the raspberries in a small bowl with a fork until the juice runs. Scoop out the passion fruit pulp into a separate bowl with the cream cheese and sugar and combine thoroughly.

COOK'S TIP

Overripe, slightly soft fruit can also be used in this recipe. You could use frozen raspberries when fresh are not available, but thaw them first.

3 Decorate each dessert with a whole raspberry and a sprig of fresh mint. Serve chilled.

VARIATION

Other summer fruits would be just as delicious – try a mix of strawberries and red currants with the raspberries, or use mangoes, peaches or apricots, which you will need to purée in a food processor or blender before mixing with the cream cheese.

2 Spoon alternating spoonfuls of the raspberry pulp and the cream cheese mixture into stemmed glasses or one large serving dish, stirring lightly to create a swirled effect.

Raspberry Muesli Layer

As well as being a delicious, low-fat, high-fiber dessert, this can also be served for a quick, healthy breakfast.

Serves 4

1⅓ cups fresh or thawed frozen
   raspberries
1 cup low-fat plain yogurt
¾ cup Swiss-style muesli

3 Sprinkle a generous layer of muesli over the yogurt.

4 Repeat with the raspberries and other ingredients. Top each with a whole raspberry.

1 Reserve four raspberries for decoration, and then spoon a few raspberries into four stemmed glasses or glass dishes.

2 Top the raspberries with a spoonful of yogurt in each glass.

COOK'S TIP

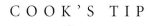

This recipe can be made in advance and stored in the fridge for several hours or overnight, if you're serving it for breakfast.

Almost Instant Banana Pudding

Banana and ginger make a great combination in this very fast dessert.

INGREDIENTS

Serves 6–8

4 thick slices gingerbread

6 bananas

2 tablespoons lemon juice

1¼ cups whipping cream or ricotta cheese

¼ cup fruit juice

2–3 tablespoons brown sugar

1 Break up the gingerbread into chunks and arrange in an ovenproof dish. Slice the bananas and toss in the lemon juice.

2 Whip the cream and, when firm, gently whip in the fruit juice. (If using ricotta, gently stir in the juice.) Fold in the bananas and spoon the mixture over the gingerbread.

3 Top with the brown sugar and place under a hot broiler for 2–3 minutes to caramelize. Chill to set firm again if desired, or serve when required.

Ginger and Orange Crème Brûlée

This is a useful way of cheating at crème brûlée! Most people would never know unless you over-chill the custard or keep it more than a day, but there's little risk of that!

INGREDIENTS

Serves 4–5

2 eggs, plus 2 egg yolks

1¼ cups light cream or half-and-half

2 tablespoons superfine sugar

1 teaspoon powdered gelatin

finely grated rind and juice of ½ orange

1 piece preserved ginger, finely chopped

3–4 tablespoons confectioners' or superfine sugar

orange and fresh mint sprig, to decorate

1 Whisk the eggs and yolks together until pale. Bring the cream and sugar to a boil, remove from the heat and sprinkle on the gelatin. Stir until the gelatin has dissolved and then pour the cream mixture onto the eggs, whisking constantly.

2 Add the orange rind, a little juice to taste, and the chopped ginger to the mixture.

3 Pour into four or five ramekins and chill until set.

4 Some time before serving, sprinkle the sugar generously over the top of the custard and put under a very hot broiler. Watch closely for the few moments it takes for the tops to caramelize. Let cool before serving. Decorate with a few segments of orange and a sprig of mint.

COOK'S TIP

For a milder ginger flavor, add up to 1 teaspoon ground ginger instead of the preserved ginger.

Pineapple Flambé

Flambéing means adding alcohol and then burning it off so the flavor is not too overpowering. This recipe is just as good, however, without the brandy – perfect if you wish to serve it to young children.

INGREDIENTS

Serves 4

1 large ripe pineapple

3 tablespoons unsalted butter

3 tablespoons brown sugar

¼ cup fresh orange juice

2 tablespoons brandy or vodka

¼ cup slivered almonds, toasted

1 Cut away the top and base of the pineapple. Then cut down the sides, removing all the dark "eyes" but leaving the pineapple in a good shape.

2 Cut the pineapple into thin slices and, with an apple corer, remove the hard central core.

3 In a large frying pan melt the butter, sugar and orange juice. Add the pineapple slices and cook for 1–2 minutes, turning once to coat both sides.

4 Add the brandy and light with a match immediately. Let the flames die down and then sprinkle with the toasted almonds.

Warm Pears in Cider

This is an excellent dessert for an autumn day.

INGREDIENTS

Serves 4

1 lemon

¼ cup superfine sugar

a little grated nutmeg

1 cup sweet cider

4 firm ripe pears

freshly made custard, cream or ice cream,
   to serve

1 Carefully remove the rind from the lemon with a potato peeler, leaving any white pith behind.

2 Squeeze the juice from the lemon into a saucepan, add the rind, sugar, nutmeg and cider, and heat through to dissolve the sugar.

3 Carefully peel the pears, leaving the stalks on if possible, and place them in the pan of cider. Poach the pears for 10–15 minutes, until almost tender, turning them frequently to cook evenly.

4 Transfer the pears to individual serving dishes using a slotted spoon. Simmer the liquid over high heat until it reduces slightly and becomes syrupy.

5 Pour the warm syrup over the pears, and serve immediately with freshly made custard, cream or ice cream.

COOK'S TIP

To get pears of just the right firmness, you may have to buy them slightly under-ripe and then wait a day or more. Soft pears are no good at all for this dish.

Chocolate Fudge Sundaes

They look impressive, taste fantastic and only take minutes to make.

INGREDIENTS

Serves 4

4 scoops each vanilla and coffee ice cream

2 small ripe bananas, sliced

whipped cream

toasted sliced almonds

For the sauce

¼ cup light brown sugar

½ cup light corn syrup

3 tablespoons strong black coffee

1 teaspoon ground cinnamon

5 ounces semisweet chocolate, chopped

⅓ cup whipping cream

3 tablespoons coffee liqueur (optional)

1 To make the sauce, place the sugar, syrup, coffee and cinnamon in a heavy saucepan. Bring to a boil, then boil for about 5 minutes, stirring the mixture constantly.

2 Turn off the heat and stir in the chocolate. When melted and smooth, stir in the cream and liqueur, if using. Let the sauce cool slightly. If made ahead, reheat the sauce gently until just warm.

3 Fill four glasses with one scoop each of vanilla and coffee ice cream.

4 Sprinkle the sliced bananas over the ice cream. Pour the warm fudge sauce over the bananas, then top each sundae with a swirl of whipped cream. Sprinkle toasted almonds over the cream and serve immediately.

VARIATION

Many variations are possible, using other flavors of ice cream such as strawberry, praline or chocolate. In the summer, substitute raspberries or strawberries for the bananas, and sprinkle chopped roasted hazelnuts on top instead of the sliced almonds.

Brazilian Coffee Bananas

Rich, lavish and sinful-looking, this dessert takes only about two minutes to make!

INGREDIENTS

Serves 4

4 small ripe bananas

1 tablespoon instant coffee granules or powder

2 tablespoons dark brown sugar

1 cup plain yogurt

1 tablespoon toasted sliced almonds

1 Peel and slice one banana and mash the remaining three with a fork.

2 Dissolve the coffee in 1 tablespoon of hot water and stir into the mashed bananas.

3 Spoon a little of the mashed banana mixture into four serving dishes and sprinkle with sugar. Top with a spoonful of yogurt, then repeat until all the ingredients are used up.

4 Swirl the last layer of yogurt for a marbled effect. Finish with a few banana slices and sliced almonds. Serve cold. Best eaten within about an hour of making.

VARIATION

For a special occasion, add a dash of dark rum or brandy to the bananas for extra richness.

Orange Yogurt Brûlées

A luxurious treat, but one that is much lower in fat than the classic brûlées, which are made with cream, eggs and lots of sugar.

INGREDIENTS

Serves 4

2 medium oranges

⅔ cup plain yogurt

¼ cup crème fraîche

3 tablespoons superfine sugar

2 tablespoons light brown sugar

3 Combine the two sugars and sprinkle them evenly over the tops of the dishes.

4 Place the dishes under a preheated, very hot broiler for 3–4 minutes, or until the sugar melts and turns a rich golden brown. Serve warm or cold.

1 With a sharp knife, cut away all the peel and white pith from the oranges and chop the fruit. Or, if there's time, segment the oranges, carefully removing all of the membrane.

2 Place the fruit in the bottom of four individual flameproof dishes. Combine the yogurt and crème fraîche and spoon the mixture over the oranges.

Broiled Pineapple with Rum Custard

Freshly ground black pepper may seem an unusual ingredient to put with pineapple until you realize that peppercorns are the fruit of a tropical vine. If the idea does not appeal, leave out the pepper.

INGREDIENTS

Serves 4

1 ripe pineapple
2 tablespoons butter
fresh strawberries, sliced, to serve
a few pineapple leaves, to decorate

For the sauce

1 egg
2 egg yolks
2 tablespoons superfine sugar
2 tablespoons dark rum
½ teaspoon freshly ground black pepper

1 Remove the top and bottom from the pineapple with a serrated knife. Pare away the outer skin from top to bottom, remove the core and cut into slices.

2 Preheat the broiler. Dot the pineapple slices with butter and broil for about 5 minutes.

3 To make the sauce, place all the ingredients in a bowl. Set over a saucepan of simmering water and whisk with a hand-held mixer for about 3–4 minutes, or until foamy and cooked. Sprinkle the strawberries over the pineapple, decorate with a few pineapple leaves and serve with the sauce.

COOK'S TIP

The sweetest pineapples are picked and exported when ripe. Contrary to popular belief, pineapples do not ripen well after picking. Choose fruit that smells sweet and yields to firm pressure from your thumbs.

Banana and Passion Fruit Whip

This very easy and quickly prepared dessert is delicious served with crisp shortcake or ginger cookies.

Serves 4

2 ripe bananas

2 passion fruit

6 tablespoons fromage frais or cream cheese

⅔ cup heavy cream

2 teaspoons honey

shortcake or ginger cookies, to serve

1 Peel the bananas, then mash them with a fork in a bowl to a smooth purée.

2 Halve the passion fruit and scoop out the pulp. Mix with the bananas and fromage frais. Whip the cream with the honey until it forms soft peaks.

3 Carefully fold the cream and honey mixture into the fruit mixture. Spoon into four glass dishes and serve immediately with shortcake.

Cinnamon and Apricot Soufflés

Don't expect this to be difficult just because it's a soufflé – it really couldn't be easier, and, best of all, it's very low in calories.

INGREDIENTS

Serves 4

3 eggs

½ cup apricot fruit spread

finely grated rind of ½ lemon

1 teaspoon ground cinnamon

extra cinnamon, to decorate

1 Preheat the oven to 375°F. Lightly grease four individual soufflé dishes and dust them lightly with flour.

2 Separate the eggs and place the yolks in a bowl with the fruit spread, lemon rind and cinnamon.

3 Whisk hard until the mixture is thick and pale in color.

4 Place the egg whites in a clean bowl and whisk them until they form soft peaks.

5 Using a metal spoon or spatula, fold the egg whites evenly into the yolk mixture.

6 Divide the soufflé mixture between the prepared dishes and bake for 10–15 minutes, until risen and golden brown. Serve immediately, dusted with a little extra ground cinnamon.

LOW
CALORIE

Fresh Citrus Gelatin

Fresh fruit gelatins really are worth the effort – they're packed with fresh flavor, natural color and vitamins – and they make a lovely fat-free dessert.

Serves 4

3 medium oranges

1 lemon

1 lime

⅓ cup superfine sugar

1 envelope powdered gelatin

extra slices of fruit, to decorate

1 With a sharp knife, cut all the peel and white pith from one orange and carefully remove the segments. Arrange the segments in the base of a 4-cup mold or dish.

2 Remove some shreds of citrus rind with a zester and reserve them for decoration. Grate the remaining rind from the lemon and lime and one orange. Place all the grated rind in a pan, with the sugar and 1¼ cups water.

3 Heat gently until the sugar has dissolved, without boiling. Remove from the heat. Squeeze the juice from all the rest of the fruit and stir it into the pan.

4 Strain the liquid into a measuring cup to remove the rind (you should have about 2½ cups: If necessary, make up the amount with water). Sprinkle the gelatin over the liquid and stir until it has completely dissolved.

5 Pour a little of the gelatin over the orange segments and chill until set. Leave the remaining gelatin at room temperature to cool, but do not let it set.

6 Pour the remaining cooled gelatin into the dish and chill until set. To serve, turn out the gelatin and decorate it with the reserved citrus rind shreds and slices of citrus fruit.

Mandarins in Orange Flower Syrup

Mandarins, tangerines, clementines, mineolas: Any of these citrus fruits are suitable for this recipe.

INGREDIENTS

Serves 4

10 mandarins
1 tablespoon confectioners' sugar
2 teaspoons orange flower water
1 tablespoon chopped pistachios

1 Thinly pare a little of the colored rind from one mandarin and cut it into fine shreds for decoration. Squeeze the juice from two mandarins and reserve it.

2 Peel the remaining fruit, removing as much of the white pith as possible. Arrange the whole fruits in a wide dish.

3 Mix the reserved juice, sugar and orange flower water and pour it over the fruit. Cover the dish and chill for at least 1 hour.

4 Blanch the shreds of rind in boiling water for 30 seconds. Drain, let cool and sprinkle them over the mandarins, with the pistachios, to serve.

COOK'S TIP

The mandarins look very attractive if you leave them whole, especially if there is a large quantity for a special occasion, but you may prefer to separate the segments.

Minted Raspberry Bavarian Cream

A sophisticated dessert that can be made a day in advance for a special dinner party.

INGREDIENTS

Serves 6

2⅔ cups fresh or thawed frozen
   raspberries

2 tablespoons confectioners' sugar

2 tablespoons lemon juice

1 tablespoon finely chopped fresh mint,
   plus fresh mint sprigs, to decorate

2 envelopes powdered gelatin

1¼ cups custard, made with skim milk

1 cup plain yogurt

1 Reserve a few raspberries for decoration. Place the raspberries, confectioners' sugar and lemon juice in a blender or food processor and process until smooth.

2 Press the purée through a sieve to remove the seeds. Add the chopped mint. You should have about 2½ cups purée.

3 Sprinkle 1 teaspoon of the gelatin over 2 tablespoons boiling water and stir until the gelatin has dissolved. Stir into ⅔ cup of the fruit purée.

4 Pour this gelatin mixture over 2 tablespoons into a 4-cup mold, and let the mold chill in the fridge until the gelatin is just on the verge of setting. Rotate the mold to swirl the setting gelatin around the sides, and then let chill until the gelatin has set completely.

5 Stir the remaining fruit purée into the custard and yogurt. Dissolve the rest of the gelatin in 3 tablespoons boiling water and stir it into the custard mixture quickly.

6 Pour the raspberry custard into the mold and let it chill until it has set completely. To serve, dip the mold quickly into hot water and then turn it out and decorate it with the reserved raspberries and the mint sprigs.

Fruited Rice Ring

This unusual rice pudding looks beautiful turned out of a ring mold, but if you prefer, stir the fruit into the rice and serve the dessert in individual dishes.

Serves 4

5 tablespoons short grain rice

3¾ cups low-fat milk

1 cinnamon stick

1 cup mixed dried fruit

¾ cup orange juice

3 tablespoons superfine sugar

finely grated rind of 1 small orange

1 Place the rice, milk and cinnamon stick in a large pan and bring to a boil. Cover and simmer, stirring occasionally, for about 1½ hours, until no liquid remains.

2 Meanwhile, place the fruit and orange juice in a pan and bring to a boil. Cover and simmer very gently for about 1 hour, until tender and no free liquid remains.

3 Remove the cinnamon stick from the rice and stir in the sugar and orange rind.

4 Turn the fruit into the bottom of a lightly oiled 6-cup ring mold. Spoon the rice over it, smoothing down firmly. Chill until needed.

5 Run a knife around the edge of the mold and turn out the rice carefully onto a serving plate.

Cherry Crêpes

These crêpes are virtually fat-free and lower in calories and higher in fiber than traditional ones. Serve with a spoonful of plain yogurt or fromage frais.

INGREDIENTS

Serves 4

½ cup all-purpose flour

½ cup whole-wheat flour

pinch of salt

1 egg white

⅔ cup skim milk

a little oil for frying

For the filling

1 can (16 ounces) dark cherries in juice

1½ teaspoons arrowroot

2 Make a well in the center of the flour and add the egg white. Gradually beat in the milk and ⅔ cup water, whisking hard until all the liquid is incorporated and the batter is smooth and bubbly.

5 Drain the cherries, reserving the juice. Blend about 2 tablespoons of the juice with the arrowroot in a saucepan. Stir in the rest of the juice. Heat gently, stirring, until boiling. Stir over medium heat for about 2 minutes, until thickened and clear.

1 Sift the flours and salt into a bowl, adding any bran left in the sieve to the bowl at the end.

3 Heat a nonstick pan with a small amount of oil until the pan is very hot. Pour in just enough batter to cover the bottom of the pan, swirling the pan to cover the bottom evenly.

4 Cook until the crêpe is set and golden and then turn to cook the other side. Remove to a sheet of absorbent paper and cook the remaining batter to make about eight crêpes.

6 Add the cherries and stir until thoroughly heated. Spoon the cherries into the crêpes and fold them into quarters.

> ## COOK'S TIP
> ～
>
> The basic crêpes will freeze very successfully, to use in future recipes. Stack the crêpes, separating them with waxed paper. Wrap in plastic and seal well in a plastic bag. Freeze for up to six months. Thaw at room temperature.

Apple Foam with Blackberries

This light dessert provides a good contrast in flavor, texture and color.

INGREDIENTS

Serves 4

8 ounces blackberries

⅔ cup apple juice

1 teaspoon powdered gelatin

1 tablespoon honey

2 egg whites

1 Place the blackberries in a pan with ¼ cup of the apple juice and heat gently until the fruit is soft. Remove from the heat, cool and chill.

2 Sprinkle the gelatin over the remaining apple juice in another pan and stir over low heat until dissolved. Stir in the honey.

3 Whisk the egg whites in a bowl until they hold stiff peaks. Continue whisking hard and pour in the hot gelatin mixture gradually, until well mixed.

4 Quickly spoon the foam into rough mounds on individual plates. Chill. Serve with the blackberries and juice spooned around.

VARIATION

Any seasonal berries can be used to accompany the apple if blackberries are not available.

COOK'S TIP

Make sure that you dissolve the gelatin over very low heat. It must not boil, or it will lose its setting ability.

Cappuccino Coffee Cups

Coffee-lovers will love this one – and it tastes rich and creamy, even though it's very light.

Serves 4

2 eggs

1 cup low-fat evaporated milk

1½ tablespoons instant coffee granules
   or powder

2 tablespoons superfine sugar

2 teaspoons powdered gelatin

¼ cup light crème fraîche

cocoa powder or ground cinnamon,
   to decorate

1 Separate one egg and reserve the white. Beat the yolk with the whole remaining egg.

2 Put the evaporated milk, coffee granules, sugar and beaten eggs in a pan; whisk until evenly combined.

3 Put the pan over low heat and stir constantly until the mixture is hot, but not boiling. Cook, stirring constantly, without boiling, until the mixture is slightly thickened and smooth.

4 Remove the pan from the heat. Sprinkle the gelatin over the pan and whisk until the gelatin has completely dissolved.

5 Spoon the coffee custard into four individual dishes or glasses and chill them until set.

6 Whisk the reserved egg white until stiff. Whisk in the crème fraîche and then spoon the mixture over the desserts. Sprinkle with cocoa or cinnamon and serve.

VARIATION

Plain yogurt can be used instead of the crème fraîche, if desired.

Summer Fruit Salad Ice Cream

What could be more cooling on a hot day than fresh summer fruits, lightly frozen in this irresistible ice?

INGREDIENTS

Serves 6

5 cups mixed summer fruit, such as raspberries, strawberries, black currants, red currants, etc.

2 eggs

1 cup plain yogurt

¾ cup red grape juice

1 envelope powdered gelatin

1 Reserve half the fruit and purée the rest in a blender or food processor, or rub it through a sieve to make a smooth purée.

2 Separate the eggs and whisk the yolks and the yogurt into the fruit purée.

3 Heat the grape juice until it's almost boiling, then remove it from the heat. Sprinkle the gelatin over the juice and stir to dissolve the gelatin completely.

4 Whisk the dissolved gelatin mixture into the fruit purée and then pour the mixture into a freezer container. Freeze until half-frozen and slushy in consistency.

5 Whisk the egg whites until they are stiff. Quickly fold them into the half-frozen mixture.

6 Return to the freezer and freeze until almost firm. Scoop into individual dishes or glasses and add the reserved berries.

Plum and Port Sorbet

This is a grown-up sorbet, but you could use fresh red grape juice instead of port if you wish to leave out the alcohol.

INGREDIENTS

Serves 4–6

2 pounds ripe red plums, halved and
    pitted
6 tablespoons superfine sugar
3 tablespoons ruby port or red wine
crisp, sweet cookies, to serve

1 Place the plums in a pan with the sugar and 3 tablespoons water. Stir over low heat until the sugar is melted, then cover and simmer gently for about 5 minutes, until the fruit is soft.

2 Put into a blender or food processor and purée until smooth, then stir in the port. Cool completely, then transfer to a freezer container and freeze until firm around the edges.

3 Spoon into the food processor and process until smooth. Return to the freezer and freeze until solid.

4 Let soften slightly at room temperature for 15–20 minutes before serving in scoops, with crisp cookies.

Tofu Berry Cheesecake

This summery cheesecake is a very light and refreshing finish to any meal. Strictly speaking, it's not a cheesecake at all, as it's based on tofu – but who would guess?

INGREDIENTS

Serves 6

¼ cup low-fat margarine

2 tablespoons apple juice

6 cups bran flakes or other high-
   fiber cereal

For the filling

1¼ cups tofu or low-fat soft cheese

1 cup low-fat plain yogurt

1 envelope powdered gelatin

4 tablespoons apple juice

For the topping

1¾ cups mixed fresh summer berries, e.g.
   strawberries, raspberries, red currants,
   blackberries, etc. (or mixed frozen
   berries)

2 tablespoons red currant jelly

1 For the shell, place the margarine and apple juice in a pan and heat gently until the margarine has melted. Crush the cereal and stir it into the pan.

2 Transfer into a 9-inch round tart pan and press down firmly. Let set.

3 For the filling, place the tofu and yogurt in a blender or food processor and process them until smooth. Dissolve the gelatin in the apple juice and stir the juice immediately into the tofu mixture.

4 Spread the tofu mixture over the chilled shell, smoothing it evenly. Place in the fridge until the filling has set.

5 Remove the tart pan and place the cheesecake on a serving plate.

6 Arrange the fruits over the top. Melt the red currant jelly with 2 tablespoons hot water. Let it cool and then spoon it over the fruit to serve.

COOK'S TIP

The lowest-calorie breakfast cereals are usually those that are highest in fiber, so it's worth checking the labels for comparisons.

Floating Islands in Hot Plum Sauce

A low-fat version of the French classic that is simpler to make than it looks. The plum sauce can be made in advance and reheated just before you cook the meringues.

INGREDIENTS

Serves 4

1 pound red plums

1¼ cups apple juice

2 egg whites

2 tablespoons apple juice concentrate

freshly grated nutmeg, to serve

1 Halve the plums and remove the pits. Place them in a wide pan, with the apple juice.

2 Bring to a boil and then cover with a lid and let simmer gently for 20–30 minutes or until the plums are tender.

3 Place the egg whites in a clean, dry bowl and whisk them until they hold soft peaks.

4 Gradually whisk in the apple juice concentrate, whisking until the meringue holds fairly firm peaks.

5 Using a tablespoon, scoop the meringue mixture into the gently simmering plum sauce. You may need to cook the "islands" in two batches.

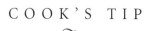

COOK'S TIP

A bottle of apple juice concentrate is a useful sweetener to keep on hand, but if you don't have any, use a little honey instead.

6 Cover and let simmer gently for 2–3 minutes, until the meringues are just set. Serve immediately, sprinkled with a little freshly grated nutmeg.

Grilled Nectarines with Ricotta and Spice

This easy dessert is good at any time of year – use canned peach halves if fresh ones are not available.

INGREDIENTS

Serves 4

4 ripe nectarines or peaches

1 tablespoon light brown sugar

½ cup ricotta cheese or
   fromage frais

½ teaspoon ground star anise

1 Cut the nectarines in half and remove the pits.

2 Arrange the nectarines, cut-side up, in a wide flameproof dish or on a baking sheet.

3 Stir the sugar into the ricotta. Using a teaspoon, spoon the mixture into the hollow of each nectarine half.

4 Sprinkle with the star anise. Place under a medium hot broiler for 6–8 minutes or until the nectarines are hot and bubbling. Serve warm.

COOK'S TIP

Star anise has a warm, rich flavor – if you can't get it, try ground cloves or pumpkin pie spice instead.

Chocolate Vanilla Timbales

*The occasional chocolate treat
doesn't do any harm, especially if it's
a dessert as light as this one.*

Serves 6

1½ cups low-fat milk

2 tablespoons cocoa powder

2 eggs

1 teaspoon vanilla extract

3 tablespoons superfine sugar

1 envelope powdered gelatin, or
    alternative

fresh mint sprig, to decorate

For the sauce

½ cup low-fat plain yogurt

½ teaspoon vanilla extract

extra cocoa powder, to sprinkle

1 Place the milk and cocoa in a
saucepan and stir until the
milk is boiling. Separate the eggs
and beat the egg yolks with the
vanilla and sugar in a bowl, until
the mixture is pale and smooth.
Gradually pour in the chocolate
milk, beating well.

2 Return the mixture to the pan
and stir constantly over gentle
heat, without boiling, until it's
slightly thickened and smooth.
Dissolve the gelatin in
3 tablespoons hot water and then
quickly stir it into the milk
mixture. Let cool until it's on the
verge of setting.

3 Whisk the egg whites until
they hold soft peaks. Fold the
egg whites quickly into the milk
mixture. Spoon the timbale
mixture into six individual molds
and chill until set.

4 To serve, run a knife around
the edge, dip the molds
quickly into hot water and turn
out the chocolate timbales onto
serving plates and decorate with a
sprig of mint. For the sauce, stir
together the yogurt and vanilla,
spoon onto the plates and sprinkle
with a little more cocoa powder.

Fluffy Banana and Pineapple Mousse

This light, low-fat mousse looks very impressive but is really very easy to make, especially with a food processor. To make it even simpler, use a 4-cup serving dish that will hold all the mixture without a paper collar.

INGREDIENTS

Serves 6

2 ripe bananas

1 cup cottage cheese

1 can (15 ounces) pineapple chunks or pieces in juice

1 envelope powdered gelatin

2 egg whites

1 Tie a double band of waxed paper around a 2½-cup soufflé dish, to come 2 inches above the rim.

2 Peel and chop one of the bananas and place it in a blender or food processor with the cottage cheese. Process until smooth.

3 Drain the pineapple, reserving the juice, and reserve a few pieces or chunks for decoration. Add the rest to the mixture in the blender or processor and process for a few seconds, until finely chopped.

4 Dissolve the gelatin in ¼ cup of the reserved pineapple juice. Stir the gelatin quickly into the fruit mixture.

5 Whisk the egg whites until they hold soft peaks and fold them into the mixture. Turn the mousse mixture into the prepared dish, smooth the surface and chill until set.

6 When the mousse is set, carefully remove the paper collar and decorate with the reserved banana and pineapple.

Greek Honey and Lemon Cake

The semolina in this recipe gives the cake an excellent texture.

INGREDIENTS

Makes 16 slices

3 tablespoons canola margarine

¼ cup honey

finely grated rind and juice of 1 lemon

⅔ cup skim milk

1¼ cups all-purpose flour

1½ teaspoons baking powder

½ teaspoon grated nutmeg

⅓ cup semolina

2 egg whites

2 teaspoons sesame seeds

1 Preheat the oven to 400°F. Lightly oil an 8-inch square deep cake pan and line the bottom with waxed paper.

2 Place the margarine and 3 tablespoons of the honey in a saucepan and heat gently until melted. Reserve 1 tablespoon lemon juice, then stir in the rest with the lemon rind and milk.

3 Stir together the flour, baking powder and nutmeg, then beat in with the semolina. Whisk the egg whites until they form soft peaks, then fold evenly into the semolina mixture.

4 Spoon into the pan and sprinkle with sesame seeds. Bake for 25–30 minutes, until golden brown.

5 Mix the reserved honey and lemon juice and drizzle over the cake while warm. Cool in the pan, then cut into bars to serve.

Strawberry Roulade

An attractive and delicious cake, perfect for a family supper.

INGREDIENTS

Serves 6

4 egg whites

scant ⅔ cup superfine sugar

⅔ cup all-purpose flour, sifted

2 tablespoons orange juice

superfine sugar, for sprinkling

1 cup strawberries, chopped, plus some strawberries, to decorate

¾ cup low-fat fromage frais or cream cheese

1 Preheat the oven to 400°F. Oil a 9 x 13-inch jelly roll pan and line with waxed paper.

2 Place the egg whites in a large, clean bowl and whisk until they form soft peaks. Gradually whisk in the sugar. Fold in half the sifted flour, then fold in the rest with the orange juice.

3 Spoon the mixture into the prepared pan, spreading evenly. Bake for 15–18 minutes, or until it is golden brown and firm to the touch.

4 Meanwhile, spread out a sheet of waxed paper and sprinkle with superfine sugar. Turn out the cake onto this and remove the lining paper. Roll up the cake loosely from one short side, with the paper inside. Cool.

5 Unroll and remove the paper. Stir the strawberries into the fromage frais and spread over the cake. Roll up and serve decorated with strawberries.

Apricot and Orange Roulade

This elegant dessert is very good served with a spoonful of plain yogurt or crème fraîche.

INGREDIENTS

Serves 6

4 egg whites

scant ⅔ cup superfine sugar

½ cup all-purpose flour

finely grated rind of 1 small orange

3 tablespoons orange juice

For the filling

½ cup dried apricots

⅔ cup orange juice

2 teaspoons confectioners' sugar, to sprinkle

orange zest, to decorate

1 Preheat the oven to 400°F. Grease a 9 x 13-inch jelly roll pan and line it with waxed paper. Grease the paper.

COOK'S TIP

Make and bake the cake mixture a day in advance and keep it, rolled with the paper, in a cool place. Fill it with the fruit purée 2–3 hours before serving. The cake can also be frozen for up to 2 months: Thaw it at room temperature and fill it as above.

2 To make the roulade, place the egg whites in a large, clean bowl and whisk them until they hold soft peaks. Gradually add the sugar, whisking vigorously between each addition.

3 Fold in the flour, orange rind and juice. Spoon the mixture into the prepared pan and spread it evenly.

4 Bake for 15–18 minutes or until the cake is firm and light golden in color. Turn out on a sheet of waxed paper and roll it up loosely from one short side. Let cool.

5 Coarsely chop the apricots and place them in a pan with the orange juice. Cover the pan and let simmer until most of the liquid has been absorbed. Purée in a blender or food processor.

6 Unroll the roulade and spread with the apricot mixture. Roll up, arrange strips of paper diagonally across the roll, sprinkle lightly with lines of confectioners' sugar, remove the paper and sprinkle with orange zest to serve.

Filo Chiffon Pie

Filo pastry is low in fat and is very easy to use. Keep a package in the freezer, ready to make impressive desserts like this one.

INGREDIENTS

Serves 3

1¼ pounds rhubarb

1 teaspoon pumpkin pie spice

finely grated rind and juice of 1 orange

1 tablespoon superfine sugar

1 tablespoon butter

3 sheets filo pastry

1 Preheat the oven to 400°F. Trim the leaves and ends from the rhubarb stalks and chop them in 1-inch pieces. Place them in a bowl.

2 Add the pumpkin pie spice, orange rind and juice and sugar, and toss well to coat evenly. Turn the rhubarb into a 4-cup pie pan.

3 Melt the butter and brush it over the pastry sheets. Lift the pastry sheets onto the pie pan, butter-side up, and crumple them to form a chiffon effect, covering the pie completely.

4 Place the dish on a baking sheet and bake it for 20 minutes, until golden brown. Reduce the heat to 350°F and bake for another 10–15 minutes, until the rhubarb is tender. Serve warm.

VARIATION

Other fruits, such as apples, pears or peaches, can be used in this pie – try it with whatever is in season.

Gooseberry Crisp

Gooseberries are perfect for traditional family desserts like this one. When they are out of season, other fruits, such as apples, plums or rhubarb, could be used instead.

INGREDIENTS

Serves 4

5 cups gooseberries

¼ cup superfine sugar

scant 1 cup rolled oats

⅔ cup whole-wheat flour

¼ cup sunflower oil

¼ cup raw sugar

2 tablespoons chopped walnuts

plain yogurt, to serve

1 Preheat the oven to 400°F. Place the gooseberries in a pan with the superfine sugar. Cover the pan and cook over low heat for 10 minutes, until the gooseberries are just tender. Transfer into an ovenproof dish.

2 To make the topping, place the oats, flour and oil in a bowl and stir with a fork until evenly mixed.

3 Stir in the raw sugar and walnuts, then spread evenly over the gooseberries. Bake for 25–30 minutes or until golden and bubbling. Serve hot with yogurt.

COOK'S TIP

The best gooseberries to use for cooking are the early, small, firm green ones.

Spiced Date and Walnut Cake

A classic flavor combination that makes a very easy, low-fat, high-fiber cake.

Makes 1 cake

2¾ cups whole-wheat self-rising flour

2 teaspoons pumpkin pie spice

1 cup chopped dates

½ cup chopped walnuts

¼ cup sunflower oil

½ cup dark brown sugar

1¼ cups skim milk

walnut halves, to decorate

1 Preheat the oven to 350°F. Grease and line a 2-pound loaf pan with waxed paper.

2 Sift together the flour and spice, then add any bran left in the sieve. Stir in the dates and walnuts.

3 Mix the oil, sugar and milk, then stir evenly into the dry ingredients. Spoon into the prepared pan and arrange the walnut halves on top.

4 Bake the cake for about 45–50 minutes or until golden brown and firm. Turn out the cake, remove the lining paper and let cool on a wire rack.

VARIATION

Pecans can be used instead of the walnuts in this cake.

Banana Orange Loaf

For the best banana flavor and a really good, moist texture, make sure the bananas are very ripe.

INGREDIENTS

Makes 1 loaf

generous ¾ cup whole-wheat flour

generous ¾ cup all-purpose flour

1 teaspoon baking powder

1 teaspoon ground pumpkin pie spice

3 tablespoons chopped hazelnuts, toasted

2 large ripe bananas

1 egg

2 tablespoons sunflower oil

2 tablespoons honey

finely grated rind and juice of 1 small orange

4 orange slices, halved

2 teaspoons confectioners' sugar

1 Preheat the oven to 350°F. Brush a 4-cup loaf pan with sunflower oil and line the bottom with waxed paper.

2 Sift the flours with the baking powder and spice into a bowl.

3 Stir the hazelnuts into the dry ingredients. Peel and mash the bananas. Beat in the egg, oil, honey and the orange rind and juice. Stir evenly into the dry ingredients.

4 Spoon into the prepared pan and smooth the top. Bake for 40–45 minutes or until firm and golden brown. Turn out and cool on a wire rack.

5 Sprinkle the orange slices with the confectioners' sugar and broil until golden. Use to decorate the cake.

COOK'S TIP

If you plan to keep the loaf for more than two or three days, omit the orange slices. Brush the cake with honey and sprinkle with chopped hazelnuts.

Banana Gingerbread

This improves with keeping. Store it in a covered container for up to two months.

INGREDIENTS

Makes 12 squares

1¾ cups all-purpose flour

2 teaspoons baking soda

2 teaspoons ground ginger

1¼ cups rolled oats

¼ cup dark brown sugar

6 tablespoons canola margarine

⅔ cup light corn syrup

1 egg, beaten

3 ripe bananas, mashed

¾ cup confectioners' sugar

preserved ginger, to decorate

1 Preheat the oven to 325°F. Grease and line a 7 x 11-inch cake pan.

2 Sift together the flour, baking soda and ginger, then stir in the rolled oats. Melt the sugar, margarine and syrup in a saucepan, then stir into the flour mixture. Beat in the egg and mashed bananas.

3 Spoon into the pan and bake for about 1 hour or until firm to the touch. Let cool in the pan, then turn out and cut into squares.

4 Sift the confectioners' sugar into a bowl and stir in just enough water to make a smooth, runny glaze. Drizzle the glaze over each square and top with pieces of preserved ginger, if desired.

COOK'S TIP

This is a nutritious cake, ideal for packed lunches, as it doesn't break up too easily.

FRUIT
DESSERTS

Cherries Jubilee

Fresh cherries are wonderful cooked lightly to serve hot over ice cream. Children will love this dessert.

INGREDIENTS
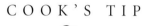

Serves 4

1 pound red or black cherries

generous ½ cup granulated sugar

pared rind of 1 lemon

1 tablespoon arrowroot

¼ cup Kirsch

vanilla ice cream, to serve

COOK'S TIP

If you don't have a cherry pitter, simply push the pits through with a skewer. Remember to save the juice to use in the recipe.

1 Pit the cherries over a pan to catch the juice. Drop the pits into the pan as you work.

2 Add the sugar, lemon rind and 1¼ cups water to the pan. Stir over low heat until the sugar dissolves, then bring to a boil and simmer for 10 minutes. Strain the syrup, then return to the pan. Add the cherries and cook for 3–4 minutes.

3 Blend the arrowroot to a paste with 1 tablespoon cold water and stir into the cherries, after removing them from the heat.

4 Return the pan to the heat and bring to a boil, stirring constantly. Cook the sauce for a minute or two, until it is thick and smooth. Heat the Kirsch in a ladle over a flame, ignite it and pour it over the cherries. Spoon the cherries and sauce over scoops of ice cream and serve immediately.

Apricots in Marsala

Make sure the apricots are completely covered by the syrup so they don't discolor.

INGREDIENTS

Serves 4

12 apricots

¼ cup superfine sugar

1¼ cups Marsala

2 strips pared orange rind

1 vanilla pod, split

⅔ cup heavy or whipping cream

1 tablespoon confectioners' sugar

¼ teaspoon ground cinnamon

⅔ cup plain yogurt

1 Halve and pit the apricots, then place in a bowl of boiling water for about 30 seconds. Drain well, then slip off their skins.

2 Place the superfine sugar, Marsala, orange rind, vanilla pod and 1 cup water in a pan. Heat gently until the sugar dissolves. Bring to a boil, without stirring, then simmer for 2–3 minutes.

3 Add the apricot halves to the pan and poach for 5–6 minutes or until just tender. Using a slotted spoon, transfer the apricots to a serving dish.

4 Boil the syrup rapidly until reduced by half, then pour over the apricots and let cool. Cover and chill. Remove the orange rind and vanilla pod.

5 Whip the cream with the confectioners' sugar and cinnamon until it forms soft peaks. Fold in the yogurt. Serve in a bowl with apricots.

Poached Pears in Red Wine

This makes a very pretty dessert, as the pears take on a red blush from the wine.

INGREDIENTS

Serves 4

1 bottle red wine

¾ cup superfine sugar

3 tablespoons honey

juice of ½ lemon

1 cinnamon stick

1 vanilla bean, split lengthwise

2-inch piece orange rind

1 clove

1 black peppercorn

4 firm ripe pears

whipped cream or sour cream, to serve

1 Place the wine, sugar, honey, lemon juice, cinnamon stick, vanilla bean, orange rind, clove and peppercorn in a saucepan just large enough to hold the pears standing upright. Heat gently, stirring occasionally until the sugar has completely dissolved.

2 Meanwhile, peel the pears, leaving the stem intact. Take a thin slice off the base of each pear so it will stand square and upright in the pan.

3 Place the pears in the wine mixture, then simmer, uncovered, for 20–35 minutes, depending on size and ripeness, until the pears are just tender; be careful not to over-cook.

4 Carefully transfer the pears to a bowl, using a slotted spoon. Continue to boil the poaching liquid until reduced by about half. Let cool, then strain the cooled liquid over the pears and chill for at least 3 hours.

5 Place the pears in four individual serving dishes and spoon a little of the red wine syrup over them. Serve with whipped or sour cream.

Hot Bananas with Rum and Raisins

Choose almost-ripe bananas with evenly colored skins, either all yellow or just green at the tips. Overripe bananas will not hold their shape well when cooked.

INGREDIENTS

Serves 4

scant ¼ cup seedless raisins

5 tablespoons dark rum

¼ cup unsalted butter

¼ cup light brown sugar

4 ripe bananas, peeled and halved
   lengthwise

¼ teaspoon grated nutmeg

¼ teaspoon ground cinnamon

2 tablespoons slivered almonds, toasted

chilled cream or vanilla ice cream, to serve
   (optional)

1 Put the raisins in a bowl with the rum. Let them soak for about 30 minutes to plump up.

2 Melt the butter in a frying pan, add the sugar and stir until dissolved. Add the bananas and cook for a few minutes, until they are tender.

3 Sprinkle the spices over the bananas, then pour in the rum and raisins. Carefully set alight using a long match, and stir gently to mix.

4 Sprinkle on the slivered almonds and serve immediately with chilled cream or vanilla ice cream, if desired.

Blueberry Pancakes

These are a lot like thick breakfast pancakes – though they can, of course, be eaten at any time.

Makes 6–8

1 cup self-rising flour

pinch of salt

3–4 tablespoons superfine sugar

2 eggs

½ cup milk

1–2 tablespoons oil

1 cup fresh or frozen
   blueberries, plus extra to decorate

maple syrup, to serve

lemon wedges, to decorate

1 Sift the flour into a bowl with the salt and sugar. Beat the eggs together thoroughly. Make a well in the middle of the flour and stir in the eggs.

2 Gradually blend in a little of the milk to make a smooth batter. Then whisk in the rest of the milk and whisk for 1–2 minutes. Let rest for 20–30 minutes.

COOK'S TIP

Instead of blueberries you could use blackberries or raspberries. If you use canned fruit, make sure it is very well drained.

3 Heat a few drops of oil in a griddle or heavy frying pan until just hazy. Pour in about 2 tablespoons of the batter and swirl the batter around until it makes an even shape.

4 Cook for 2–3 minutes and, when almost set on top, sprinkle 1–2 tablespoons blueberries on it. As soon as the bottom is loose and golden brown, turn the pancake over.

5 Cook on the second side for only about 1 minute, until golden and crisp. Slide the pancake onto a plate and serve drizzled with maple syrup. Continue with the rest of the batter. Serve decorated with lemon wedges and a few extra blueberries.

Rhubarb-Strawberry Crisp

Strawberries, cinnamon and ground almonds make this a luxurious and delicious version of plain rhubarb crisp.

INGREDIENTS

Serves 4

8 ounces strawberries, hulled

1 pound rhubarb, diced

½ cup sugar

1 tablespoon cornstarch

⅓ cup fresh orange juice

1 cup all-purpose flour

1 cup rolled oats

½ cup light brown sugar,
   firmly packed

½ teaspoon ground cinnamon

½ cup ground almonds

generous ½ cup cold butter

1 egg, lightly beaten

1 If the strawberries are large, cut them in half. Combine the strawberries, rhubarb and sugar in a 10-cup baking dish. Preheat the oven to 350°F.

2 In a small bowl, blend the cornstarch with the orange juice. Pour this mixture over the fruit and stir gently to coat. Set the baking dish aside while making the crumb topping.

3 In a bowl, toss together the flour, oats, brown sugar, cinnamon and ground almonds. With a pastry blender or two knives, cut in the butter until the mixture resembles coarse bread crumbs. Stir in the beaten egg.

4 Spoon the oat mixture evenly over the fruit and press down gently. Bake until browned, 50 minutes to 1 hour, then serve warm.

Fruit Kebabs with Mango and Yogurt Sauce

These mixed fresh fruit kebabs make an attractive and healthy dessert.

INGREDIENTS

Serves 4

½ pineapple, peeled, cored and cubed

2 kiwi fruit, peeled and cubed

1½ cups strawberries, hulled and cut in half, if large

½ mango, peeled, pitted and cubed

For the sauce

½ cup fresh mango purée, from 1–1½ peeled and pitted mangoes

½ cup thick plain yogurt

1 teaspoon superfine sugar

few drops vanilla extract

1 tablespoon finely chopped fresh mint leaves

1 To make the sauce, beat together the mango purée, yogurt, sugar and vanilla with an electric mixer.

2 Stir in the chopped mint. Cover the sauce and place in the fridge until required.

3 Thread the prepared fruit onto twelve 6-inch wooden skewers, alternating the pineapple, kiwi fruit, strawberries and mango cubes.

4 Arrange the kebabs on a large serving tray with the mango and yogurt sauce in the center.

Tropical Fruits in Cinnamon Syrup

An exotic glazed fruit salad is a simply prepared but satisfying end to any meal.

INGREDIENTS

Serves 6

2¼ cups superfine sugar

1 cinnamon stick

1 large or 2 medium papayas (about 1½ pounds), peeled, seeded and cut lengthwise into thin pieces

1 large or 2 medium mangoes (about 1½ pounds), peeled, pitted and cut lengthwise into thin pieces

1 large or 2 small star fruit (about 8 ounces), thinly sliced

yogurt or crème fraîche, to serve

1 Sprinkle one-third of the sugar over the bottom of a large saucepan. Add the cinnamon stick and half the papaya, mango and star fruit pieces.

2 Sprinkle half of the remaining sugar over the fruit pieces in the pan. Add all the remaining fruit and sprinkle with the rest of the sugar.

3 Cover the pan and cook the fruit over medium-low heat for 35–45 minutes, until the sugar melts completely. Shake the pan occasionally, but do not stir or the fruit will collapse.

4 Uncover the pan and simmer until the fruit begins to appear translucent, about 10 minutes. Remove the pan from the heat and let cool.

5 Transfer the fruit and syrup to a bowl, cover and chill overnight. Serve with yogurt or crème fraîche.

Mango Sorbet

A light and refreshing dessert that's surprisingly easy to make.

INGREDIENTS

Serves 6

¾ cup superfine sugar

a large strip of orange rind

1 large mango, peeled, pitted and cubed

¼ cup orange juice

fresh mint sprigs, to decorate

1 Combine the sugar, orange rind and ¾ cup water in a saucepan. Bring to a boil, stirring to dissolve the sugar. Let the syrup cool.

2 Purée the mango cubes with the orange juice in a blender or food processor. There should be about 2 cups of purée.

3 Add the purée to the cooled sugar syrup and mix well. Strain, then chill.

4 When cold, transfer into a freezer container and freeze until firm around the edges.

5 Spoon the semi-frozen mixture into the food processor and process until smooth. Return to the freezer and freeze until solid. Let the sorbet soften slightly at room temperature for 15–20 minutes before serving, decorated with mint sprigs.

VARIATIONS

For Banana Sorbet: Peel and cube 4–5 large bananas. Purée with 2 tablespoons lemon juice to make 2 cups. If desired, replace the orange rind in the sugar syrup with 2–3 whole cloves, or omit the rind.

For Papaya Sorbet: Peel, seed and cube 1½ pounds papaya. Purée with 3 tablespoons lime juice to make 2 cups. Replace the orange rind with lime rind.

For Passion Fruit Sorbet: Halve 16 or more passion fruit and scoop out the seeds and pulp (there should be about 2 cups). Work in a blender or food processor until the seeds are like coarse pepper. Omit the orange juice and rind. Add the passion fruit to the sugar syrup, then press through a wire sieve before freezing.

Raspberry Trifle

Use fresh or frozen raspberries for this ever-popular desert.

INGREDIENTS

Serves 6 or more

6 ounces trifle sponges or plain Victoria
   sponge, cut into 1-inch cubes, or
   coarsely crumbled ladyfingers
¼ cup medium sherry
4 ounces raspberry jam
1⅔ cups raspberries
scant 2 cups custard, flavored with
   2 tablespoons medium or sweet sherry
1¼ cups sweetened whipped cream
toasted sliced almonds and mint leaves,
   to decorate

1 Spread half of the sponges, cake cubes or ladyfingers over the bottom of a large serving bowl. (A glass bowl is best for presentation.)

2 Sprinkle half of the sherry over the cake to moisten it. Spoon on half of the jam, dotting it evenly over the cake cubes.

3 Reserve a few raspberries for decoration. Make a layer of half the remaining raspberries on top.

4 Pour on half of the custard, covering the fruit and cake. Repeat the layers. Cover and chill for at least 2 hours.

5 Before serving, spoon the sweetened whipped cream evenly over the top. To decorate, sprinkle with toasted sliced almonds and arrange the reserved raspberries and mint leaves on the top.

VARIATION

Use other ripe summer fruits such as apricots, peaches, nectarines and strawberries in the trifle, with jam and liqueur to taste.

Apple Fritters

Make sure you buy plenty of apples for this recipe. They taste so good you'll probably have to cook an extra batch.

INGREDIENTS

Serves 4–6

1⅓ cups all-purpose flour

2 teaspoons baking powder

¼ teaspoon salt

⅔ cup milk

1 egg, beaten

oil for deep-frying

¾ cup sugar

1 teaspoon ground cinnamon

2 large tart-sweet apples, peeled, cored, and cut in ¼-inch slices

confectioners' sugar, for dusting

1 Sift the flour, baking powder and salt into a bowl. Beat in the milk and egg with a wire whisk.

2 Heat at least 3 inches of oil in a heavy frying pan to 360°F or until a cube of bread browns in 1–2 minutes.

3 Mix the sugar and cinnamon in a shallow bowl or plate. Toss the apple slices in the sugar mixture to coat all over.

4 Dip the apple slices in the batter, using a fork or slotted spoon. Drain off excess batter. Fry in batches in the hot oil, until golden brown on both sides, about 4–5 minutes. Drain the fritters on paper towels.

5 Sprinkle with confectioners' sugar, and serve hot.

Cherry Compote

Sweet cherries in syrup to serve with cream or ice cream.

INGREDIENTS

Serves 6

½ cup red wine

¼ cup light brown sugar, firmly packed

¼ cup granulated sugar

1 tablespoon honey

1-inch strips of orange rind

¼ teaspoon almond extract

1½ pounds fresh sweet cherries, pitted

ice cream or whipped cream, for serving

1 Combine all the ingredients except the cherries and ice cream or whipped cream in a saucepan with ½ cup water. Stir over medium heat until the sugar dissolves. Raise the heat and boil until the liquid reduces slightly.

2 Add the cherries. Bring back to a boil. Reduce the heat slightly and simmer for 8–10 minutes. If necessary, skim off any foam.

3 Let cool to lukewarm. Spoon warm over vanilla ice cream, or refrigerate and serve cold with whipped cream, if desired.

Clementines in Cinnamon Caramel

The combination of sweet yet sharp clementines and caramel sauce with a hint of spice is divine. Served with plain yogurt or crème fraîche, this makes a delicious dessert.

INGREDIENTS

Serves 4–6

8–12 clementines
generous 1 cup sugar
2 cinnamon sticks
2 tablespoons orange-flavored liqueur
¼ cup shelled pistachios

1 Pare the rind from two clementines using a vegetable peeler and cut it into fine strips. Set aside.

2 Peel the clementines, removing all the pith but keeping them intact. Put the fruit in a serving bowl.

3 Gently heat the sugar in a pan until it melts and turns a rich golden brown. Immediately turn off the heat.

4 Cover your hand with a dish-towel and pour in 1¼ cups warm water (the mixture will bubble and splutter). Bring slowly to a boil, stirring until the caramel has dissolved. Add the shredded peel and cinnamon sticks, then simmer for 5 minutes. Stir in the orange-flavored liqueur.

5 Let the syrup cool for about 10 minutes, then pour it over the clementines. Cover the bowl and chill for several hours or overnight.

6 Blanch the pistachios in boiling water. Drain, cool and remove the dark outer skins. Sprinkle them over the clementines and serve immediately.

Chocolate Amaretti Peaches

Quick and easy to prepare, this delicious dessert can also be made with fresh nectarines or apricots.

INGREDIENTS

Serves 4

4 ounces amaretti cookies, crushed

2 ounces semisweet chocolate, chopped

grated rind of ½ orange

1 tablespoon honey

¼ teaspoon ground cinnamon

1 egg white, lightly beaten

4 firm ripe peaches

⅔ cup white wine

1 tablespoon superfine sugar

whipped cream, to serve

1 Preheat the oven to 375°F. Combine the crushed amaretti cookies, chocolate, orange rind, honey and cinnamon in a bowl. Add the beaten egg white and mix to bind the mixture together.

2 Halve and pit the peaches and fill the cavities with the chocolate mixture, mounding it up slightly.

3 Arrange the stuffed peaches in a lightly buttered, shallow ovenproof dish that will just hold the peaches comfortably. Pour the wine into a measuring cup and stir in the sugar.

4 Pour the wine mixture around the peaches. Bake for 30–40 minutes, until the peaches are tender. Serve immediately with a little of the cooking juices spooned over and the whipped cream.

Fruity Ricotta Creams

Ricotta is an Italian soft cheese with a smooth texture and a mild, slightly sweet flavor. Served here with candied fruit peel and delicious chocolate – it is quite irresistible.

INGREDIENTS

Serves 4

1½ cups ricotta cheese

2–3 tablespoons Cointreau or other orange liqueur

2 teaspoons grated lemon rind

2 tablespoons confectioners' sugar

⅔ cup heavy cream

scant 1 cup candied peel, such as orange, lemon and citron, finely chopped

2 ounces semisweet chocolate, finely chopped

chocolate curls, to decorate

amaretti cookies, to serve (optional)

1 Using the back of a wooden spoon, push the ricotta through a fine sieve into a large bowl.

2 Add the liqueur, lemon rind and confectioners' sugar to the ricotta and beat well until the mixture is light and smooth.

3 Whip the cream in a large bowl until it forms soft peaks.

4 Gently fold the cream into the ricotta mixture with the candied peel and chopped chocolate.

5 Spoon the mixture into four glass serving dishes and chill for about 1 hour. Decorate the ricotta creams with chocolate curls and serve with amaretti cookies, if desired.

Hot Fruit with Maple Butter

Turn exotic fruits into comfort food by grilling them with maple syrup and butter.

INGREDIENTS

Serves 4

1 large mango

1 large papaya

1 small pineapple

2 bananas

½ cup unsalted butter

¼ cup pure maple syrup

ground cinnamon, for sprinkling

COOK'S TIP

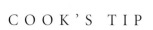

Prepare the fruit just before broiling to prevent it from discoloring.

1 Peel the mango and cut the flesh into large pieces. Halve the papaya and scoop out the seeds. Cut into thick slices, then peel away the skin.

2 Peel and core the pineapple and slice into thin wedges. Peel the bananas, then halve them lengthwise.

3 Cut the butter into small dice and place in a blender or food processor with the maple syrup, then process until the mixture is smooth and creamy.

4 Place the mango, papaya, pineapple and banana on a broiler rack and brush with the maple syrup butter.

5 Cook the fruit under medium heat for about 10 minutes, until just tender, turning the fruit occasionally and brushing it with the butter.

6 Arrange the fruit on a warmed serving platter and dot with the remaining butter. Sprinkle on a little ground cinnamon and serve the fruit piping hot.

Ruby Fruit Salad

After a rich main course, this port-flavored fruit salad is light and refreshing. Use any combination of fruit that is available.

INGREDIENTS

Serves 8

½ cup superfine sugar

1 cinnamon stick

4 cloves

pared rind of 1 orange

1¼ cups port

2 oranges

1 small ripe cantaloupe or honeydew melon

4 small bananas

2 apples

8 ounces seedless grapes

1 Put the sugar, spices, pared orange rind and 1¼ cups water into a pan and stir over gentle heat to dissolve the sugar. Then bring to a boil, cover with a lid and simmer for 10 minutes. Let cool, then add the port.

2 Strain the liquid (to remove the spices and orange rind) into a bowl. With a sharp knife, cut off all the skin and pith from the oranges. Then, holding each orange over the bowl to catch the juice, cut away the segments by slicing between the membrane that divides each segment and letting the segments drop into the syrup. Squeeze the remaining pith to release any juice.

3 Cut the melon in half, remove the seeds and scoop out the flesh with a melon baller, or cut it in small cubes. Add it to the syrup.

4 Peel the bananas and cut them diagonally in ½-inch slices. Quarter and core the apples and cut them in small cubes. Leave the skin on, or peel them if it is tough. Halve the grapes if large or leave them whole. Stir all the fruit into the syrup, cover with plastic wrap and chill for 1 hour before serving.

Summer Pudding

Unbelievably simple to make and totally delicious, this is a real warm-weather classic.

INGREDIENTS

Serves 4

about 8 thin slices day-old white bread, crusts removed

1¼ pounds mixed summer fruits

2 tablespoons sugar

1 Cut a round from one slice of bread to fit in the bottom of a 5-cup pudding mold, then cut strips of bread about 2 inches wide to line the mold, overlapping the strips.

2 Gently heat the fruit, sugar and 2 tablespoons water in a large heavy saucepan, shaking the pan occasionally, until the juices begin to run.

3 Reserve about 3 tablespoons fruit juice, then spoon the fruit and remaining juice into the mold, taking care not to dislodge the bread lining.

4 Cut the remaining bread to fit entirely over the fruit. Stand the basin on a plate and cover with a saucer or small plate that will just fit inside the top of the mold. Place a heavy weight on top. Chill the pudding and the reserved fruit juice overnight.

5 Run a knife carefully around the inside of the mold rim, then invert the pudding onto a cold serving plate. Pour the reserved juice over the pudding and serve.

COOK'S TIP

Summer pudding freezes well, so make an extra one to enjoy during the winter.

Banana Honey Yogurt Ice

Using yogurt instead of cream gives this cool dessert a more refreshing, less sugary taste.

INGREDIENTS

Serves 4–6

4 ripe bananas, coarsely chopped

1 tablespoon lemon juice

2 tablespoons honey

generous 1 cup plain yogurt

½ teaspoon ground cinnamon

crisp cookies, chopped hazelnuts and
   banana slices, to serve

1 Place the bananas in a food
processor or blender with the
lemon juice, honey, yogurt and
cinnamon. Process until smooth
and creamy.

2 Pour the mixture into a freezer
container and freeze until
almost solid. Spoon back into the
food processor and process again
until smooth.

3 Pour back into the freezer
container and freeze until
firm. Let soften at room
temperature for 15 minutes, then
serve with crisp cookies, chopped
hazelnuts and banana slices.

VARIATION

To make Banana Maple Yogurt Ice,
use maple syrup instead of honey.

Autumn Pudding

*As its name suggests, this is a tasty
seasonal variation of summer
pudding using apples, blackberries
and plums.*

INGREDIENTS

Serves 6

10 slices white or brown bread, at least
   one day old

1 Cortland apple, peeled, cored and sliced

8 ounces ripe red plums, halved and pitted

8 ounces blackberries

6 tablespoons superfine sugar

low-fat yogurt or fromage frais, to serve

1 Remove the crusts from the
bread and use a cookie cutter
to stamp out a 3-inch round from
one slice. Cut the remaining slices
in half.

2 Place the bread round on the
bottom of a 5-cup pudding
mold, then overlap the fingers
around the sides, saving some for
the top.

3 Place the apple, plums,
blackberries, sugar and
¼ cup water in a pan, heat gently
until the sugar dissolves, then
simmer for 10 minutes, until soft.
Remove from the heat.

4 Reserve the juice and spoon
the fruit into the bread-lined
mold. Top with the reserved bread,
then gently spoon on the reserved
fruit juices.

5 Cover the mold with a saucer
and place weights on top. Chill
the pudding overnight. Turn out
onto a serving plate and serve with
low-fat yogurt or fromage frais.

COOK'S TIP

Choose good-quality bread that
is not too thinly sliced – it needs
to be at least ¼ inch thick so it
supports the fruit when the
pudding is turned out.

Ruby Plum Mousse

*Red plums and port give this mousse
its delicate flavor and color.*

INGREDIENTS

Serves 6

1 pound ripe red plums

3 tablespoons granulated sugar

¼ cup ruby port

1 envelope powdered gelatin

3 eggs, separated

generous ½ cup superfine sugar

⅔ cup heavy cream

skinned and chopped pistachios, to
    decorate

cinnamon cookies, to serve (optional)

1 Place the plums and
   granulated sugar in a pan with
2 tablespoons water. Cook over
low heat until softened. Press the
fruit through a sieve to remove the
pits and skins. Let cool, then stir in
the port.

2 Put 3 tablespoons water in a
   small bowl, sprinkle the gelatin
over it and let soften. Stand the
bowl in a pan of hot water and let
stand until dissolved. Stir into the
plum purée.

3 Place the egg yolks and
   superfine sugar in a bowl and
whisk until thick and mousse-like.
Fold in the plum purée, then whip
the cream and fold in gently.

4 Whisk the egg whites until
   they hold stiff peaks, then
carefully fold in using a metal
spoon. Divide among six glasses
and chill until set.

5 Decorate each mousse with
   chopped pistachios and
serve with crisp cinnamon
cookies, if desired.

Warm Autumn Compote

*An easily prepared dessert with a
sophisticated taste.*

INGREDIENTS

Serves 4

6 tablespoons superfine sugar

1 bottle red wine

1 vanilla bean, split

1 strip pared lemon rind

4 pears

2 purple figs, quartered

1⅓ cups raspberries

lemon juice, to taste

1 Put the sugar and wine in a
   large pan and heat gently until
the sugar is dissolved. Add the
vanilla bean and lemon rind and
bring to a boil, then simmer
for 5 minutes.

2 Peel and halve the pears, then
   scoop out the cores, using a
melon baller. Add the pears to the
syrup and poach for 15 minutes,
turning the pears several times so
they color evenly.

3 Add the figs and poach for
   another 5 minutes, until the
fruits are tender.

4 Transfer the poached pears
   and figs to a serving bowl
using a slotted spoon, then
sprinkle on the raspberries.

5 Return the syrup to the heat
   and boil rapidly to reduce
slightly and concentrate the flavor.
Add a little lemon juice to taste.
Strain the syrup over the fruits and
serve warm.

Apricot and Pear Filo Strudel

This is a very quick way of making a strudel – normally, they are very time consuming to make – but it tastes delicious!

Serves 4–6

½ cup dried apricots, chopped

2 tablespoons apricot jam

1 teaspoon lemon juice

¼ cup light brown sugar

2 medium pears, peeled, cored and chopped

½ cup ground almonds

2 tablespoons slivered almonds

2 tablespoons butter

8 sheets filo pastry

confectioners' sugar, to dust

1 Put the apricots, apricot jam, lemon juice, brown sugar and pears into a pan and heat gently, stirring, for 5–7 minutes.

2 Remove from the heat and cool. Mix in the ground and slivered almonds. Preheat the oven to 400°F. Melt the butter.

3 Lightly grease a baking sheet. Layer the pastry on the baking sheet, brushing each layer with the melted butter.

4 Spoon the filling onto the pastry on one side of the center and within 1 inch of each end. Lift the other side of the pastry up by sliding a spatula underneath.

5 Fold this pastry over the filling, tucking the edge under. Seal the ends neatly and brush all over with butter again.

6 Bake for 15–20 minutes, until golden. Dust with confectioners' sugar and serve hot.

Red Berry Tart with Lemon Cream Filling

This tart is best filled just before serving so the pastry remains mouth-wateringly crisp. Select red berries such as strawberries, raspberries or red currants.

INGREDIENTS

Serves 6–8

1¼ cups all-purpose flour

¼ cup cornstarch

5 tablespoons confectioners' sugar

7 tablespoons butter

1 teaspoon vanilla extract

2 egg yolks, beaten

fresh mint sprig, to decorate

For the filling

scant 1 cup cream cheese

3 tablespoons lemon curd

grated rind and juice of 1 lemon

confectioners' sugar, to sweeten (optional)

2 cups mixed red berries

3 tablespoons red currant jelly

1 Sift the flour, cornstarch and confectioners' sugar together, then rub in the butter until the mixture resembles bread crumbs.

2 Beat the vanilla into the egg yolks, then mix into the crumbs to make a firm dough, adding cold water if necessary.

3 Roll out the pastry and line a 9-inch round tart pan, pressing the dough up the sides after trimming. Prick the shell of the tart with a fork and let it rest in the fridge for 30 minutes.

4 Preheat the oven to 400°F. Line the shell with waxed paper and baking beans. Place the pan on a baking sheet and bake for 20 minutes, removing the paper and beans for the last 5 minutes. When cooked, cool and remove the pastry shell from the tart pan.

5 Cream the cheese, lemon curd and lemon rind and juice, adding confectioners' sugar to sweeten, if desired. Spread the mixture into the tart shell.

6 Top the tart with the fruits. Gently warm the red currant jelly and trickle it over the fruits just before serving, decorated with a fresh mint sprig.

VARIATIONS

There are all sorts of delightful variations to this recipe. For instance, leave out the red currant jelly and sprinkle lightly with confectioners' sugar or decorate with fresh strawberry leaves. Alternatively, top with sliced kiwi fruit or banana slices sprinkled with lemon juice.

Ginger Baked Pears

This simple French dessert is the kind that would be served after Sunday lunch or a family supper. Try to find Comice or Anjou pears – this recipe can be made with slightly underripe fruit.

INGREDIENTS

Serves 4

4 large pears

1¼ cups whipping cream

¼ cup superfine sugar

½ teaspoon vanilla extract

¼ teaspoon ground cinnamon

pinch of freshly grated nutmeg

1 teaspoon grated fresh ginger

1 Preheat the oven to 375°F. Lightly butter a large shallow baking dish.

2 Peel the pears, cut in half lengthwise and remove the cores. Arrange, cut-side down, in a single layer in the baking dish.

3 Combine the cream, sugar, vanilla extract, cinnamon, nutmeg and ginger and pour it over the pears.

4 Bake for 30–35 minutes, basting occasionally, until the pears are tender and browned on top and the cream is thick and bubbly. Cool slightly before serving.

Prunes Poached in Red Wine

Serve this simple dessert on its own, or with crème fraîche or vanilla ice cream.

INGREDIENTS

Serves 8–10

1 unwaxed orange

1 unwaxed lemon

3 cups fruity red wine

¼ cup superfine sugar, or to taste

1 cinnamon stick

pinch of freshly grated nutmeg

2 or 3 cloves

1 teaspoon black peppercorns

1 bay leaf

2 pounds large pitted prunes, soaked in cold water

cream, to serve

strips of orange rind, to decorate

1 Using a vegetable peeler, peel two or three strips of rind from both the orange and lemon. Squeeze the juice from both and put in a large saucepan.

2 Add the wine, sugar, spices, peppercorns, bay leaf and strips of rind to the pan with 2 cups water.

3 Bring to a boil over medium heat, stirring occasionally to dissolve the sugar. Drain the prunes and add to the saucepan, reduce the heat to low and simmer, covered, for 10–15 minutes, until the prunes are tender. Remove from the heat and set aside until cool.

4 Using a slotted spoon, transfer the prunes to a serving dish. Return the cooking liquid to medium-high heat, and bring to a boil. Boil for 5–10 minutes, until slightly reduced and syrupy, then pour or strain over the prunes. Cool, then chill before serving with cream, decorated with strips of orange rind, if desired.

Apple Soufflé Omelet

Apples sautéed until they are slightly caramelized make a delicious autumn filling – you could also use fresh raspberries or strawberries when they are in season.

INGREDIENTS

Serves 2

4 eggs, separated

2 tablespoons light cream or half-and-half

1 tablespoon superfine sugar

1 tablespoon butter

confectioners' sugar, for dredging

For the filling

1 apple, peeled, cored and sliced

2 tablespoons butter

2 tablespoons light brown sugar

3 tablespoons light cream or half-and-half

1 To make the filling, sauté the apple slices in the butter and sugar until just tender. Stir in the cream and keep warm while making the omelet.

2 Place the egg yolks in a bowl with the cream and sugar and beat well. Whisk the egg whites until they form stiff peaks, then fold into the yolk mixture.

3 Melt the butter in a large heavy frying pan, pour in the soufflé mixture and spread evenly. Cook for 1 minute until golden underneath, then cover the pan handle with foil and place under a broiler to brown the top.

4 Slide the omelet onto a plate, add the apple mixture, then fold over. Sift the confectioners' sugar over thickly, then mark in a crisscross pattern with a hot metal skewer. Serve immediately.

Blackberry Cobbler

Make the most of the fresh autumn blackberries with this juicy dessert.

Serves 8

6 cups blackberries

1 cup granulated sugar

3 tablespoons all-purpose flour

grated rind of 1 lemon

2 tablespoons sugar mixed with
   ¼ teaspoon grated nutmeg

For the topping

2 cups all-purpose flour

1 cup sugar

1 tablespoon baking powder

pinch of salt

1 cup milk

½ cup butter, melted

1 Preheat the oven to 350°F. In a bowl, combine the blackberries, sugar, flour and lemon rind. Stir gently to blend. Transfer to a 2-quart baking dish.

2 For the topping, sift the flour, sugar, baking powder and salt into a large bowl. In a large cup, combine the milk and butter.

3 Gradually stir the milk mixture into the dry ingredients, and stir until the batter is just smooth.

4 Spoon the batter over the berries, spreading to the edges.

5 Sprinkle the surface with the sugar and nutmeg mixture. Bake until the batter topping is set and lightly browned, about 50 minutes. Serve hot.

COOK'S TIP

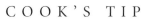

If desired, use half blackberries and half raspberries or strawberries for the filling.

Greek Fig and Honey Pudding

A quick and easy dessert made from fresh or canned figs topped with thick and creamy plain yogurt, drizzled with honey and sprinkled with pistachios.

INGREDIENTS

Serves 4

4 fresh or canned figs

2 cups plain strained yogurt

¼ cup honey

2 tablespoons chopped pistachios

1 Chop the figs and place in the bottom of four stemmed wine glasses or deep, individual dessert bowls.

2 Top each glass or bowl of figs with ½ cup of the plain yogurt. Chill until ready to serve.

3 Just before serving, drizzle 1 tablespoon honey over each one and sprinkle with the pistachios.

> ### COOK'S TIP
> Try specialty honeys made from clover, acacia or thyme blossoms.

Russian Fruit Compote

This fruit pudding is traditionally called "Kissel" and is made from the thickened juice of stewed red or black currants. This recipe uses the whole fruit with an added dash of blackberry liqueur.

INGREDIENTS

Serves 4

2 cups red or black currants or a mixture of both

1⅓ cups raspberries

¼ cup superfine sugar

1½ tablespoons arrowroot

1–2 tablespoons blackberry liqueur

plain yogurt, to serve

> ### COOK'S TIP
> Use crème de cassis instead of blackberry liqueur.

1 Place the red or black currants, raspberries and sugar in a pan with ⅔ cup water. Cover the pan and cook gently over low heat for 12–15 minutes, until the fruit is soft.

2 Blend the arrowroot with a little water in a bowl and stir into the fruit. Bring back to a boil, stirring until thickened.

3 Remove from the heat and cool slightly, then gently stir in the blackberry liqueur.

4 Pour into four serving bowls and leave until cold, then chill. Serve topped with spoonfuls of plain yogurt.

Spiced Red Fruit Compote

An aromatic and colorful dessert to serve on a cold day.

Serves 4

4 ripe red plums, halved

2 cups strawberries, halved

1⅓ cups raspberries

2 tablespoons light brown sugar

1 cinnamon stick

3 pieces star anise

6 cloves

plain yogurt, to serve

1 Place the plums, strawberries and raspberries in a heavy pan with the sugar and 2 tablespoons cold water.

2 Add the cinnamon stick, star anise and cloves to the pan and heat gently, without boiling, until the sugar dissolves and the fruit juices run.

3 Cover the pan and let the fruit infuse over very low heat for about 5 minutes. Remove the spices from the compote before serving warm with plain yogurt.

Rhubarb Spiral Cobbler

Orange in the fruit filling and in the topping gives this cobbler added zest.

Serves 4

1½ pounds rhubarb, sliced

¼ cup superfine sugar

3 tablespoons orange juice

For the topping

1⅓ cups self-rising flour

2 tablespoons superfine sugar

1 cup plain yogurt

grated rind of 1 medium orange

2 tablespoons raw sugar

1 teaspoon ground ginger

yogurt, to serve

1 Preheat the oven to 400°F. Cook the rhubarb, sugar and orange juice in a covered pan until tender. Transfer into an ovenproof dish.

2 To make the topping, mix the flour and superfine sugar, then stir in enough of the yogurt to bind to a soft dough.

3 Roll out on a floured surface to a 10-inch square. Mix the orange rind, raw sugar and ginger, then sprinkle this over the surface of the dough.

4 Roll up quite tightly, then cut into about ten slices using a sharp knife. Arrange the slices over the rhubarb.

5 Bake in the oven for 15–20 minutes, or until the spirals are well risen and golden brown. Serve warm, with yogurt.

CAKES, PIES
AND TARTS

~

Chocolate Layer Cake

The cake layers can be made ahead, wrapped and frozen for future use. Always defrost cakes completely before icing.

INGREDIENTS

Serves 10–12

unsweetened cocoa for dusting

1 can (8 ounces) cooked whole beets, drained and juice reserved

½ cup unsalted butter, softened

2½ cups light brown sugar, firmly packed

3 eggs

1 tablespoon vanilla extract

3 ounces unsweetened chocolate, melted

2¼ cups all-purpose flour

2 teaspoons baking powder

½ teaspoon salt

½ cup buttermilk

chocolate curls (optional)

For the chocolate ganache frosting

2 cups whipping or heavy cream

1¼ pounds fine quality bittersweet or semisweet chocolate, chopped

1 tablespoon vanilla extract

1 Preheat the oven to 350°F. Grease two 9-inch cake pans and dust bottom and sides with cocoa. Grate the beets and add to the beet juice. With an electric mixer, beat the butter, brown sugar, eggs and vanilla until pale and fluffy (3–5 minutes). Reduce the speed and beat in the chocolate.

2 In a bowl, sift the flour, baking powder and salt. With the mixer on low speed, alternately beat in the flour mixture in fourths and the buttermilk in thirds. Add the beets and juice and beat for 1 minute. Divide between pans and bake for 30–35 minutes or until a cake tester inserted in the center comes out clean. Cool for 10 minutes, then unmold and cool completely.

3 Heat the cream in a heavy saucepan over medium heat, stirring occasionally to prevent it from scorching, until it just begins to boil.

4 Remove from the heat and stir in the chocolate, stirring constantly until melted and smooth. Stir in the vanilla. Strain into a bowl and refrigerate, stirring every 10 minutes, until spreadable, about 1 hour.

5 Assemble the cake. Place one layer on a serving plate and spread with one-third of the ganache. Turn the cake layer bottom side up and spread the remaining ganache over the top and sides of the cake. If using, top with the chocolate curls. Let the frosting set for 20–30 minutes, then refrigerate before serving.

Marbled Jelly Roll

Simply sensational – that's the combination of light chocolate cake and walnut chocolate buttercream.

INGREDIENTS

Serves 6–8

scant 1 cup all-purpose flour

1 tablespoon cocoa powder

1 ounce semisweet chocolate, grated

1 ounce white chocolate, grated

3 eggs

generous ½ cup superfine sugar

For the filling

6 tablespoons unsalted butter or
    margarine, softened

1½ cups confectioners' sugar

1 tablespoon cocoa powder

½ teaspoon vanilla extract

3 tablespoons chopped walnuts

plain and white chocolate curls, to
    decorate (optional)

1 Preheat the oven to 400°F. Grease a 12 x 8-inch jelly roll pan and line with waxed paper. Sift half the flour with the cocoa into a bowl. Stir in the grated semisweet chocolate. Sift the remaining flour into another bowl; stir in the grated white chocolate.

2 Whisk the eggs and sugar in a heatproof bowl; set over a saucepan of hot water until the mixture holds its shape when the whisk is lifted.

3 Remove the bowl from the heat and transfer half the mixture into a separate bowl. Fold the white chocolate mixture into one portion, then fold the semisweet chocolate mixture into the other. Stir 1 tablespoon boiling water into each half to soften the mixtures.

4 Place alternate spoonfuls of the mixture in the prepared pan and swirl lightly together for a marbled effect. Bake for about 12–15 minutes or until firm. Turn out onto a sheet of waxed paper.

5 Trim the edges to neaten and cover with a damp, clean dish-towel. Cool.

6 For the filling, beat the butter or margarine, confectioners' sugar, cocoa powder and vanilla extract together in a bowl until smooth, then mix in the walnuts.

7 Uncover the sponge, lift off the waxed paper and spread the surface with the buttercream. Roll up carefully from a long side and place on a serving plate. Decorate with plain and white chocolate curls, if desired.

Sponge Cake with Fruit and Cream

Called génoise, this is the French cake used as the base for both simple and elaborate creations. You could simply dust it with confectioners' sugar, or layer it with seasonal fruits to serve as a seasonal dessert.

INGREDIENTS

Serves 6

1 cup all-purpose flour

pinch of salt

4 eggs, at room temperature

scant ⅔ cup superfine sugar

½ teaspoon vanilla extract

¼ cup butter, melted or clarified and cooled

For the filling

1 pound fresh strawberries or raspberries

2–4 tablespoons superfine sugar

2 cups whipping cream

1 teaspoon vanilla extract

1 Preheat the oven to 350°F. Lightly butter a 9-inch springform pan or deep cake pan. Line the bottom with waxed paper, and dust lightly with flour. Sift the flour and salt together twice.

2 Half fill a medium saucepan with hot water and set over low heat (do not let the water boil). Put the eggs in a heatproof bowl that just fits into the pan without touching the water. Using an electric mixer, beat the eggs at medium-high speed, gradually adding the sugar, for 8–10 minutes, until the mixture is very thick and pale and leaves a ribbon trail when the beaters are lifted. Remove the bowl from the pan, add the vanilla extract and continue beating until the mixture is cool.

3 Fold in the flour mixture in three batches, using a balloon whisk or metal spoon. Before the third addition of flour, stir a large spoonful of the mixture into the melted or clarified butter to lighten it, then fold the butter into the remaining mixture with the last addition of flour. Work quickly but gently, so the mixture does not deflate. Pour into the prepared pan, smoothing the top so the sides are slightly higher than the center.

4 Bake for about 25–30 minutes, until the top of the cake springs back when touched and the edge begins to shrink away from the sides of the pan. Place the cake in its pan on a wire rack to cool for 5–10 minutes, then invert the cake onto the rack to cool completely. Peel off the paper.

5 To make the filling, slice the strawberries, place in a bowl, sprinkle with 1–2 tablespoons of the sugar and set aside. Beat the cream with the rest of the sugar and the vanilla extract until it holds soft peaks.

6 To assemble the cake (up to 4 hours before serving), split the cake horizontally, using a serrated knife. Place the top, cut side up, on a serving plate. Spread with a third of the cream and cover with an even layer of sliced strawberries.

7 Place the bottom half of the cake, cut side down, on top of the filling and press lightly. Spread the remaining cream over the top and sides of the cake. Chill until ready to serve. Serve the remaining strawberries with the cake.

Devil's Food Cake with Orange Frosting

Chocolate and orange are the ultimate combination. Can you resist the temptation?

Serves 8–10

½ cup unsweetened cocoa powder

¾ cup butter, at room temperature

1½ cups dark brown sugar, firmly packed

3 eggs, at room temperature

2 cups all-purpose flour

1½ tablespoons baking soda

¼ teaspoon baking powder

¾ cup sour cream

orange rind strips, for decoration

For the frosting

1½ cups granulated sugar

2 egg whites

¼ cup frozen orange juice concentrate

1 tablespoon fresh lemon juice

grated rind of 1 orange

1 Preheat the oven to 350°F. Line two 9-inch cake pans with waxed paper and grease. In a bowl, mix the cocoa and ¾ cup boiling water until smooth. Set aside.

2 With an electric mixer, cream the butter and sugar until light and fluffy. Add the eggs, one at a time, beating well.

3 When the cocoa mixture is lukewarm, stir into the butter mixture.

4 Sift together the flour, baking soda and baking powder twice. Fold into the cocoa mixture in three batches, alternating with the sour cream.

5 Pour into the pans. Bake until the cakes pull away from the pan, 30–35 minutes. Stand for 15 minutes before unmolding.

6 Thinly slice the orange rind strips. Blanch in boiling water for 1 minute.

7 For the frosting, place all the ingredients in the top of a double boiler or in a bowl set over hot water. With an electric mixer, beat until the mixture holds soft peaks. Remove from heat and beat until thick enough to spread.

8 Sandwich the cake with frosting, then spread over the top and sides. Arrange the rind on top.

Black Forest Cherry Cake

This light chocolate sponge, moistened with Kirsch and layered with cherries and cream, is still one of the most popular of all the chocolate cakes.

INGREDIENTS

Serves 8–10

6 eggs

scant 1 cup superfine sugar

1 teaspoon vanilla extract

½ cup all-purpose flour

½ cup cocoa powder

½ cup unsalted butter, melted

For the filling and topping

¼ cup Kirsch

2½ cups heavy or whipping cream

2 tablespoons confectioners' sugar

½ teaspoon vanilla extract

1½ pound jar pitted red cherries, drained

To decorate

confectioners' sugar, for dusting

grated chocolate

chocolate curls

fresh or drained canned red cherries

1 Preheat the oven to 350°F. Grease three 8-inch sandwich cake pans and line the bottom of each with waxed paper. Whisk the eggs with the sugar and vanilla extract in a large bowl until pale and very thick – the mixture should leave a ribbon trail when the whisk is lifted.

2 Sift the flour and cocoa over the mixture and fold in lightly and evenly. Stir in the melted butter. Divide the mixture among the prepared cake pans, smoothing them level.

3 Bake for 15–18 minutes, until risen and springy to the touch. Let cool in the pans for about 5 minutes, then turn out onto wire racks and let cool completely.

4 Prick each layer all over with a skewer or fork, then sprinkle with Kirsch. Whip the cream in a bowl until it starts to thicken, then beat in the confectioners' sugar and vanilla extract until the mixture begins to hold its shape.

5 To assemble, spread one cake layer with a thick layer of flavored cream and top with a quarter of the cherries. Spread a second cake layer with cream and cherries, then place it on top of the first layer. Top with the final layer.

6 Spread the remaining cream all over the cake. Dust a plate with confectioners' sugar; position the cake. Press grated chocolate over the sides and decorate with the chocolate curls and cherries.

Angel Food Cake

This cake is beautifully light. The secret? Sifting the flour over and over again to let plenty of air into it.

INGREDIENTS

Serves 12–14

1 cup sifted cake flour

1½ cups superfine sugar

1¼ cups egg whites (about 10–11 eggs)

1¼ teaspoons cream of tartar

¼ teaspoon salt

1 teaspoon vanilla extract

¼ teaspoon almond extract

confectioners' sugar, for dusting

1 Preheat the oven to 325°F. Sift the flour before measuring, then sift it four times with ½ cup of the sugar. Transfer to a bowl.

2 With an electric mixer, beat the egg whites until foamy. Sift over the cream of tartar and salt and continue to beat until they hold soft peaks when the beaters are lifted.

3 Add the remaining sugar in three batches, beating well after each addition. Stir in the vanilla and almond extract.

4 Add the flour mixture, ½ cup at a time, and fold in gently with a large metal spoon after each addition.

5 Transfer to an ungreased 10-inch straight-sided ring mold and bake until delicately browned on top, about 1 hour.

6 Turn the ring mold upside down onto a cake rack and let cool for 1 hour. If the cake does not unmold, run a spatula around the edge to loosen it. Invert onto a serving plate.

7 When cool, lay a star-shaped template on top of the cake, sift with confectioners' sugar, and lift off.

Chocolate and Cherry Polenta Cake

*Polenta and almonds add an
unusual nutty texture to this
delicious dessert.*

INGREDIENTS

Serves 8

⅓ cup quick-cooking polenta

7 ounces semisweet chocolate, broken into
  squares

5 eggs, separated

¾ cup superfine sugar

1 cup ground almonds

¼ cup all-purpose flour

finely grated rind of 1 orange

½ cup candied cherries, halved

confectioners' sugar, for dusting

1 Place the polenta in a
heatproof bowl and pour in
just enough boiling water to
cover, about ½ cup. Stir well,
then cover the bowl and let stand
for about 30 minutes, until the
polenta has absorbed all the
excess moisture.

2 Preheat the oven to 375°F.
Grease a deep 8-inch round
cake pan and line the base with
waxed paper. Melt the chocolate in
a heatproof bowl over hot water.

3 Whisk the egg yolks with the
sugar in a bowl until thick and
pale. Beat in the chocolate, then
fold in the polenta, ground
almonds, flour and orange rind.

4 Whisk the egg whites in a
clean bowl until stiff. Stir
1 tablespoon of the whites into the
chocolate mixture, then fold in the
rest. Finally, fold in the cherries.

5 Scrape the mixture into the
prepared pan and bake for
45–55 minutes, until well risen and
firm. Cool on a rack. Dust with
confectioners' sugar to serve.

Lemon Coconut Layer Cake

The flavors of lemon and coconut complement each other beautifully in this light cake.

INGREDIENTS

Serves 8–10

1 cup all-purpose flour

pinch of salt

8 eggs

1¾ cups granulated sugar

1 tablespoon grated orange rind

grated rind of 2 lemons

juice of 1 lemon

½ cup shredded coconut

2 tablespoons cornstarch

6 tablespoons butter

For the frosting

½ cup unsalted butter, at room
   temperature

1 cup confectioners' sugar

grated rind of 1 lemon

6–8 tablespoons fresh lemon juice

1 package (14 ounces) shredded coconut

1 Preheat the oven to 350°F. Line three 8-inch cake pans with waxed paper and grease them. In a bowl, sift together the flour and salt and set aside.

2 Place six of the eggs in a large heatproof bowl set over hot water. With an electric mixer, beat until frothy. Gradually beat in ¾ cup of the granulated sugar until the mixture doubles in volume and is thick enough to leave a ribbon trail when the beaters are lifted, which takes about 10 minutes.

3 Remove the bowl from the hot water. Fold in the orange rind, half the grated lemon rind and 1 tablespoon of the lemon juice until blended. Fold in the coconut.

4 Sift the flour mixture in three batches, folding in thoroughly after each addition.

5 Divide the mixture between the prepared pans.

6 Bake until the cakes pull away from the sides of the pan, 25–30 minutes. Let stand 3–5 minutes, then unmold and transfer to a cooling rack.

7 In a bowl, blend the cornstarch with a little cold water to dissolve. Whisk in the remaining eggs until just blended. Set aside.

8 In a saucepan, combine the remaining lemon rind and juice, the remaining sugar, butter and 1 cup water.

9 Over medium heat, bring the mixture to a boil. Whisk in the eggs and cornstarch, and return to a boil. Whisk constantly until thick, about 5 minutes. Remove from the heat. Cover with waxed paper to prevent a skin from forming and set aside.

10 For the frosting, cream the butter and confectioners' sugar until smooth. Stir in the lemon rind and enough lemon juice to obtain a thick, spreadable consistency.

11 Sandwich the three cake layers with the lemon custard mixture. Spread the frosting over the top and sides. Cover the cake with the coconut, pressing it in gently.

Carrot Cake with Maple Butter Frosting

A good, quick dessert cake for a family supper.

INGREDIENTS

Serves 12

1 pound carrots, peeled

1½ cups all-purpose flour

2 teaspoons baking powder

½ teaspoon baking soda

1 teaspoon salt

2 teaspoons ground cinnamon

4 eggs

2 teaspoons vanilla extract

1 cup dark brown sugar, firmly packed

½ cup granulated sugar

1¼ cups sunflower oil

1 cup walnuts, finely chopped

½ cup raisins

walnut halves, for decorating (optional)

For the frosting

6 tablespoons unsalted butter, at room
   temperature

3 cups confectioners' sugar

¼ cup maple syrup

1 Preheat the oven to 350°F. Line an 11 x 8-inch rectangular cake pan with waxed paper and grease it. Grate the carrots and set aside.

2 Sift the flour, baking powder, baking soda, salt and cinnamon into a bowl. Set aside.

3 With an electric mixer, beat the eggs until blended. Add the vanilla, sugars and oil; beat to incorporate. Add the dry ingredients in three batches, folding in well after each addition.

4 Add the carrots, walnuts and raisins and fold in thoroughly.

5 Pour the batter into the prepared pan and bake until the cake springs back when touched lightly, 40–45 minutes. Let stand 10 minutes, then unmold and transfer to a rack.

6 For the frosting, cream the butter with half the sugar until soft. Add the syrup, then beat in the remaining sugar until blended.

7 Spread the frosting over the top of the cake. Using a metal spatula, make decorative ridges in the frosting. Cut into squares. Decorate with walnut halves.

Black and White Pound Cake

A good cake for packed lunches and picnics, as it cuts into neat slices with no messy filling, or for serving with custard for dessert.

INGREDIENTS

Serves 16

4 ounces semisweet chocolate, broken into squares

3 cups all-purpose flour

1 teaspoon baking powder

2 cups butter, at room temperature

3 cups sugar

1 tablespoon vanilla extract

10 eggs, at room temperature

confectioners' sugar, for dusting

1 Preheat the oven to 350°F. Line the bottom of a 10-inch straight-sided ring mold with waxed paper and grease it. Dust with flour spread evenly with a brush.

2 Melt the chocolate in the top of a double boiler, or in a heatproof bowl set over a pan of hot water. Stir occasionally. Set aside.

3 In a bowl, sift together the flour and baking powder. In another bowl, cream the butter, sugar and vanilla extract with an electric mixer until light and fluffy. Add the eggs, two at a time, then gradually incorporate the flour mixture on low speed.

4 Spoon half of the batter into the prepared mold.

COOK'S TIP

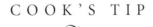

This is also known as Marble Cake because of its distinctive appearance.

5 Stir the chocolate into the remaining batter, then spoon into the mold. With a metal spatula, swirl the two batters to create a marbled effect.

6 Bake until a cake tester inserted in the center comes out clean, about 1¾ hours. Cover with foil halfway through baking. Let stand 15 minutes, then unmold and transfer to a cooling rack. To serve, dust with confectioners' sugar.

Chocolate Mousse Strawberry Layer Cake

The strawberries used in this cake can be replaced by raspberries or blackberries and the appropriate flavor liqueur.

INGREDIENTS

Serves 10

4 ounces fine quality white chocolate, chopped

½ cup whipping or heavy cream

½ cup milk

1 tablespoon rum or vanilla extract

½ cup unsalted butter, softened

generous ¾ cup granulated sugar

3 eggs

2½ cups all-purpose flour

1 teaspoon baking powder

pinch of salt

1½ pounds fresh strawberries, sliced, plus extra for decoration

For the white chocolate mousse

9 ounces fine quality white chocolate, chopped

1½ cups whipping or heavy cream

2 tablespoons rum or strawberry liqueur

For the topping

3 cups whipping cream

2 tablespoons rum or strawberry liqueur

1 Preheat the oven to 350°F. Grease and flour two 9-inch cake pans. Line the base of the pans with waxed paper. Melt the chocolate and cream in a double boiler over a low heat, stirring until smooth. Stir in the milk and 1 tablespoon rum; set aside to cool.

2 In a large bowl with an electric mixer, beat the butter and sugar until light and creamy. Add the eggs one at a time, beating well.

3 In a small bowl, stir together the flour, baking powder and salt. Alternately add flour and melted chocolate to the eggs in batches, until just blended. Pour the batter evenly into the pans.

4 Bake for 20–25 minutes, until a cake tester inserted in the center comes out clean. Cool on a wire rack for 10 minutes. Turn the cakes out onto the wire rack, peel off the paper and cool completely.

5 Prepare the mousse. In a medium saucepan over low heat, melt the chocolate and cream until smooth, stirring frequently. Stir in 2 tablespoons rum and pour into a bowl. Chill until just set. With a wire whisk, whip lightly until the mixture has a "mousse" consistency.

6 Slice both cake layers in half horizontally. Sandwich the four layers together with the mousse and strawberries.

7 To make the topping, whip the cream with the rum until firm peaks form. Spread half over the top and sides of the cake. Spoon the remaining cream into a pastry bag with a star tip and pipe scrolls on top. Garnish with strawberries.

Death by Chocolate

One of the richest chocolate cakes ever, so serve it in thin slices.

INGREDIENTS

Serves 16–20

8 ounces semisweet dark chocolate, broken into squares

½ cup unsalted butter

⅔ cup milk

1¼ cups light brown sugar

2 teaspoons vanilla extract

2 eggs, separated

⅔ cup sour cream

2 cups self-rising flour

1 teaspoon baking powder

For the filling

¼ cup seedless raspberry jam

¼ cup brandy

14 ounces semisweet dark chocolate, broken into squares

scant 1 cup unsalted butter

For the topping

1 cup heavy cream

8 ounces semisweet dark chocolate, broken into squares

plain and white chocolate curls, to decorate

chocolate-dipped physalis (Cape gooseberries), to serve (optional)

1 Preheat the oven to 350°F. Grease and line the bottom of a deep 9-inch springform cake pan. Place the chocolate, butter and milk in a saucepan. Heat gently until smooth. Remove from the heat, beat in the sugar and vanilla, then cool.

2 Beat the egg yolks and sour cream in a bowl, then beat into the chocolate mixture. Sift the flour and baking powder over the surface and fold in. Whisk the egg whites in a grease-free bowl until stiff; fold into the mixture.

3 Scrape into the prepared pan and bake for 45–55 minutes or until firm to the touch. Cool in the pan for 15 minutes, then invert onto a wire rack to cool.

4 Slice the cold cake horizontally into three even layers. In a small saucepan, warm the jam with 1 tablespoon of the brandy, then brush over two of the layers. Heat the remaining brandy in a saucepan with the chocolate and butter, stirring, until smooth. Cool until beginning to thicken.

5 Spread the bottom layer of the cake with half the chocolate filling, taking care not to disturb the jam. Top with a second layer, jam side up, and spread with the remaining filling. Top with the final layer and press lightly. Let set.

6 To make the topping, heat the cream and chocolate together in a saucepan over low heat, stirring frequently until the chocolate has melted. Pour into a bowl, let cool, then whisk until the mixture begins to hold its shape.

7 Spread the top and sides of the cake with the chocolate topping. Decorate with chocolate curls and, if desired, chocolate-dipped physalis.

Simple Chocolate Cake

An easy, everyday chocolate cake that can be filled with buttercream, or with a rich chocolate ganache for a special occasion.

INGREDIENTS

Serves 6–8

4 ounces semisweet chocolate, broken into
   squares
3 tablespoons milk
⅔ cup unsalted butter or margarine,
   softened
scant 1 cup light brown sugar
3 eggs
1¾ cups self-rising flour
1 tablespoon cocoa powder

For the buttercream

6 tablespoons unsalted butter or
   margarine, softened
1½ cups confectioners' sugar
1 tablespoon cocoa powder
½ teaspoon vanilla extract
confectioners' sugar and cocoa powder,
   for dusting

1 Preheat the oven to 350°F. Grease two 7-inch round cake pans and line the bottom of each with waxed paper. Melt the chocolate with the milk in a heatproof bowl set over a pan of simmering water.

2 Cream the butter with the sugar in a mixing bowl until pale and fluffy. Add the eggs one at a time, beating well after each addition. Stir in the chocolate mixture until it is well combined.

3 Sift the flour and cocoa over the mixture and fold in with a metal spoon until evenly mixed. Scrape into the prepared pans, smooth to level and bake for 35–40 minutes or until well risen and firm. Turn out on wire racks and let cool.

4 To make the buttercream, beat the butter, confectioners' sugar, cocoa powder and vanilla extract together in a bowl until the mixture is smooth.

5 Sandwich the cake layers together with the buttercream. Dust with a mixture of confectioners' sugar and cocoa before serving.

Pineapple Upside-Down Cake

This is a perennial favorite to serve in winter or summer.

INGREDIENTS

Serves 8

½ cup butter

1 cup dark brown sugar,
   firmly packed

1 can (16 ounces) pineapple slices,
   drained

4 eggs, separated

grated rind of 1 lemon

pinch of salt

½ cup granulated sugar

¾ cup all-purpose flour

1 teaspoon baking powder

1 Preheat the oven to 350°F. Melt the butter in an ovenproof cast-iron frying pan, about 10-inches in diameter. Remove 1 tablespoon of the melted butter and set aside.

2 Add the brown sugar to the frying pan and stir until blended. Place the drained pineapple slices on top in one layer. Set aside.

3 In a bowl, whisk together the egg yolks, reserved butter and lemon rind until smooth and well blended. Set aside.

4 With an electric mixer, beat the egg whites with the salt until stiff. Fold in the granulated sugar, 2 tablespoons at a time. Fold in the egg yolk mixture.

5 Sift the flour and baking powder together. Fold into the egg mixture in three batches.

6 Pour the batter over the pineapple and smooth level.

7 Bake until a cake tester inserted in the center comes out clean, about 30 minutes.

8 While still hot, place a serving plate on top of the frying pan, bottom-side up. Holding them together with oven gloves, flip over. Serve hot or cold.

Peach and Blueberry Pie

The unusual combination of fruits in this pie looks especially good with a lattice pastry topping.

Serves 8

2 cups all-purpose flour

pinch of salt

2 teaspoons sugar

10 tablespoons cold butter

1 egg yolk

2 tablespoons milk, to glaze

For the filling

1 pound fresh peaches, peeled, pitted
    and sliced

2 cups fresh blueberries

¾ cup superfine sugar

2 tablespoons fresh lemon juice

⅓ cup all-purpose flour

large pinch of freshly grated nutmeg

2 tablespoons butter or margarine, cut
    into tiny pieces

1 To make the pastry, sift the flour, salt and sugar into a bowl. Rub the butter into the dry ingredients as quickly as possible until the mixture resembles coarse bread crumbs.

2 Mix the egg yolk with ¼ cup ice water and sprinkle over the flour mixture. Combine with a fork until the dough holds together. If the dough is too crumbly, add a little more water, 1 tablespoon at a time. Gather the dough into a ball and flatten into a round. Place in a plastic bag, seal and chill for at least 20 minutes.

3 Roll out two-thirds of the pastry between two sheets of waxed paper to a thickness of about ⅛ inch. Use to line a 9-inch pie pan.

4 Trim the pastry all around, leaving a ½-inch overhang. Fold the overhang under to form the edge. Using a fork, press the edge to the rim of the pie pan.

5 Gather the trimmings and remaining pastry into a ball, and roll out to a thickness of about ¼ inch. Using a pastry wheel or sharp knife, cut into long, ½-inch-wide strips. Chill both the pastry shell and the strips of pastry for 20 minutes. Meanwhile, preheat the oven to 400°F.

6 Line the pastry shell with waxed paper and fill with dried beans. Bake for 7–10 minutes, until the pastry is just set. Remove from the oven and carefully lift out the paper with the beans. Prick the bottom of the pastry shell with a fork, then return to the oven and bake for another 5 minutes. Let cool slightly before filling. Leave the oven on.

7 For the filling, place the peach slices and blueberries in a bowl and stir in the sugar, lemon juice, flour and nutmeg. Spoon the fruit mixture into the pastry shell. Dot the top with the pieces of butter or margarine.

8 Weave a lattice top with the chilled pastry strips, pressing the ends to the edge of the baked pastry shell. Brush the strips with the milk.

9 Bake the pie for 15 minutes. Reduce the oven temperature to 350°F, and continue baking for another 30 minutes, until the filling is tender and bubbling and the pastry lattice is golden. If the pastry becomes too brown, cover loosely with a piece of foil. Serve the pie warm or at room temperature.

COOK'S TIP
〜
Don't over-chill the pastry strips. If they become too firm, they may crack and break as you weave them into a lattice.

Rhubarb Pie

Use a cookie cutter to cut out decorative pastry shapes and make this pie extra special.

INGREDIENTS

Serves 6

1½ cups all-purpose flour

½ teaspoon salt

2 teaspoons superfine sugar

6 tablespoons cold butter or margarine

2 tablespoons light cream or half-and-half, plus additional, to serve

For the filling

2¼ pounds fresh rhubarb, cut into 1-inch slices

2 tablespoons cornstarch

1 egg

1½ cups superfine sugar

1 tablespoon grated orange rind

1 To make the pastry, sift the flour, salt and sugar into a bowl. Using a pastry blender or two knives, cut the butter into the dry ingredients as quickly as possible until the mixture resembles bread crumbs.

2 Sprinkle the flour mixture with about ¼ cup ice water and mix until the dough just holds together. If the dough is too crumbly, add a little more water, 1 tablespoon at a time.

3 Gather the dough into a ball, flatten into a round, place in a plastic bag and put in the fridge for 20 minutes.

4 Roll out the pastry between two sheets of waxed paper to a ⅛-inch thickness. Use to line a 9-inch pie pan. Trim all around, leaving a ½-inch overhang. Fold the overhang under the edge and flute. Chill the shell and trimmings for 30 minutes.

5 To make the filling, put the rhubarb in a bowl, sprinkle with the cornstarch and toss to coat.

6 Preheat the oven to 425°F. Beat the egg with the sugar in a bowl until thoroughly blended, then mix in the orange rind.

7 Stir the sugar mixture into the rhubarb and mix well together, then spoon the fruit into the prepared pastry shell.

8 Roll out the pastry trimmings. Cut out decorative shapes with a cookie cutter.

9 Arrange the pastry shapes on top of the pie. Brush the shapes and the edge of the pastry case with cream.

10 Bake the pie for 30 minutes. Reduce the oven temperature to 325°F and continue baking for another 15–20 minutes, until the pastry is golden brown and the rhubarb is tender. Serve the pie hot with cream.

Key Lime Pie

Key limes come from Florida, but if they are not available, ordinary limes will do just as well.

Serves 8

3 large egg yolks

1 can (14 ounces) sweetened condensed
  milk

1 tablespoon grated Key lime rind

½ cup fresh Key lime juice

green food coloring (optional)

½ cup whipping cream

For the crust

1¼ cups graham cracker crumbs

5 tablespoons butter or margarine, melted

1 Preheat the oven to 350°F. For the crust, place the graham cracker crumbs in a bowl and add the butter. Stir to combine.

2 Press the crumbs evenly over the bottom and sides of a 9-inch pie plate or pan. Bake for 8 minutes. Let cool.

3 Beat the yolks until thick. Beat in the milk, lime rind and juice and coloring, if using. Pour into the pre-baked pie crust and refrigerate until set, about 4 hours. To serve, whip the cream. Pipe a lattice pattern on top, or spoon dollops around the edge.

Fruit Tartlets

The chocolate pastry shells make a dramatic base to these tartlets.

Makes 8

¾ cup red currant or grape jelly

1 tablespoon fresh lemon juice

¾ cup whipping cream

1½ pounds fresh fruit, such as
  strawberries, raspberries, kiwi fruit,
  peaches, grapes or blueberries, peeled
  and sliced as necessary

For the pastry

⅔ cup cold butter, cut in pieces

⅓ cup dark brown sugar,
  firmly packed

3 tablespoons unsweetened cocoa powder

1½ cups all-purpose flour

1 egg white

1 For the pastry, combine the butter, brown sugar and cocoa over low heat. When the butter is melted, remove from the heat and sift over the flour. Stir, then add just enough egg white to bind the mixture. Gather into a ball, wrap in waxed paper and chill for at least 30 minutes.

2 Preheat the oven to 350°F. Grease eight 3-inch tartlet pans. Roll out the dough between two sheets of waxed paper and cut out eight 4-inch rounds with a fluted cutter.

3 Line the tartlet pans with dough. Prick the bottoms. Chill for 15 minutes.

4 Bake until firm, 20–25 minutes. Let cool, then remove from the pans.

5 Melt the jelly with the lemon juice. Brush a thin layer on the bottom of the tartlets. Whip the cream and spread a thin layer in the tartlet shells. Arrange the fruit on top. Brush evenly with the glaze and serve.

Chocolate Pecan Torte

This torte uses finely ground nuts instead of flour. Toast, then cool, the nuts before grinding them finely in a blender or food processor. Do not overgrind the nuts, as the oils will form a paste.

INGREDIENTS

Serves 16

7 ounces bittersweet or semisweet
  chocolate, chopped

10 tablespoons unsalted butter, cut into
  pieces

4 eggs

½ cup superfine sugar

2 teaspoons vanilla extract

1 cup ground pecans

2 teaspoons ground cinnamon

24 toasted pecan halves to decorate
  (optional)

For the chocolate honey glaze

4 ounces bittersweet or semisweet
  chocolate, chopped

¼ cup unsalted butter, cut into pieces

2 tablespoons honey

pinch of ground cinnamon

1 Preheat the oven to 350°F. Grease an 8-inch springform pan; line with waxed paper, then grease the paper. Wrap the bottom and sides of the pan with foil to prevent water from seeping in. In a saucepan over low heat, melt the chocolate and butter, stirring until smooth. Remove from the heat. In a mixing bowl with an electric mixer, beat the eggs, sugar and vanilla extract until frothy, 1–2 minutes. Stir in the melted chocolate, ground nuts and cinnamon. Pour into the prepared pan.

2 Place the foil-wrapped pan in a large roasting pan and pour boiling water into the roasting pan, to come ¾ inch up the side of the springform pan. Bake for 25–30 minutes, until the edge of the cake is set, but the center is soft. Remove from the water bath and remove the foil. Cool on a rack.

3 Prepare the glaze. In a small saucepan over low heat, melt the chocolate, butter, honey and cinnamon, stirring until smooth; remove from the heat. Carefully dip the toasted pecan halves halfway into the glaze and place on a waxed paper-lined baking sheet until set.

4 Remove the sides from the springform pan and invert the cake onto a wire rack. Remove the pan bottom and paper, so the bottom of the cake is now the top. Pour the thickened glaze over the cake, tilting the rack slightly to spread the glaze. Use a metal spatula to smooth the sides. Arrange the glazed nuts around the outside edge of the torte and let the glaze set.

Cherry Pie

The woven lattice is the perfect finishing touch, although you can cheat and use a lattice pastry roller if you prefer.

INGREDIENTS

Serves 8

2 pounds fresh cherries, pitted, or 2
   1-pound cans or jars, drained and
   pitted
generous ¾ cup superfine sugar
¼ cup all-purpose flour
1½ tablespoons fresh lemon juice
¼ teaspoon almond extract
2 tablespoons butter or margarine

For the pastry
2 cups all-purpose flour
1 teaspoon salt
¾ cup vegetable shortening

1 For the pastry, sift the flour and salt into a mixing bowl. Using a pastry blender, cut in the shortening until the mixture resembles coarse bread crumbs.

2 Sprinkle in 4–5 tablespoons ice water, a tablespoon at a time, tossing lightly with your fingertips or a fork until the pastry forms a ball.

3 Preheat the oven to 425°F. Divide the pastry in half and shape each half into a ball. On a lightly floured surface, roll out one of the balls to a circle about 12 inches in diameter.

4 Use it to line a 9-inch pie pan, easing the pastry in and being careful not to stretch it. With scissors, trim off excess pastry, leaving a ½-inch overhang around the pie pan.

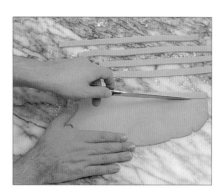

5 Roll out the remaining pastry to ⅛ inch thick. Cut out eleven strips ½ inch wide.

6 In a mixing bowl, combine the cherries, sugar, flour, lemon juice and almond extract. Spoon the mixture into the pastry case and dot the top with the butter.

7 To make the lattice, place five of the pastry strips evenly across the filling. Fold every other strip back. Lay the first strip across in the opposite direction. Continue in this pattern, folding back every other strip each time you add a cross strip.

8 Trim the ends of the lattice strips even with the shell overhang. Press together so that the edge rests on the pie-pan rim. With your thumbs, flute the edge. Chill for 15 minutes.

9 Bake the pie for 30 minutes, covering the edge of the pastry case with foil, if necessary, to prevent over-browning. Let cool, in the pan, on a wire rack.

Mince Pies with Orange Cinnamon Pastry

Homemade mince pies are so much better than store bought, especially with this tasty pastry.

INGREDIENTS

Makes 18

2 cups all-purpose flour

1½ ounces confectioners' sugar

2 teaspoons ground cinnamon

10 tablespoons cold butter

grated rind of 1 orange

⅔ cup mincemeat

1 beaten egg, to glaze

confectioners' sugar, to dust

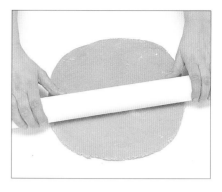

1 Sift together the flour, confectioners' sugar and cinnamon, then rub in the butter until it forms crumbs. (This can be done in a food processor.) Stir in the grated orange rind.

2 Mix to a firm dough with about ¼ cup ice water. Knead lightly, then roll out to a ¼-inch thickness.

3 Using a 2½-inch round cutter, cut out 18 circles, gathering scraps and rerolling. Then cut out 18 smaller 2-inch circles.

4 Line two muffin pans with the 18 larger circles – they will fill one and a half pans. Spoon a small spoonful of mincemeat into each pastry shell and top with the smaller pastry circles, pressing the edges lightly together to seal.

5 Glaze the tops of the pies with egg and let rest in the refrigerator for 30 minutes. Preheat the oven to 400°F.

6 Bake the pies for 15–20 minutes, until they are golden brown. Remove them to wire racks to cool. Serve just warm and dusted with confectioners' sugar.

Apple-Cranberry Lattice Pie

Use fresh or frozen cranberries for this classic autumn pie.

INGREDIENTS

Serves 8

grated rind of 1 orange

3 tablespoons fresh orange juice

2 large, tart apples

1 cup cranberries

½ cup raisins

¼ cup walnuts, chopped

1 cup granulated sugar

½ cup dark brown sugar

1 tablespoon quick-cooking tapioca

For the pastry

2 cups all-purpose flour

½ teaspoon salt

6 tablespoons cold butter, cut in pieces

¼ cup cold vegetable shortening,
   cut in pieces

about 1 tablespoon granulated sugar,
   for sprinkling

1 For the pastry, sift the flour and salt into a bowl. Add the butter and shortening and rub in until the mixture resembles coarse crumbs. With a fork, stir in just enough ice water to bind the dough. Gather into two equal balls, wrap in waxed paper and chill for at least 20 minutes.

2 Put the orange rind and juice into a mixing bowl. Peel and core the apples and grate them into the bowl. Stir in the cranberries, raisins, walnuts, granulated sugar, brown sugar and tapioca.

3 Place a baking sheet in the oven and preheat to 400°F.

4 On a lightly floured surface, roll out one ball of dough about ⅛ inch thick. Transfer to a 9-inch pie pan and trim the edge. Spoon the cranberry and apple mixture into the shell.

5 Roll out the remaining dough to a circle about 11 inches in diameter. With a serrated pastry wheel, cut the dough into ten strips, ¾ inch wide. Place five strips horizontally across the top of the tart at 1-inch intervals. Weave in six vertical strips. Trim the edges. Sprinkle the top with about 1 tablespoon of sugar.

6 Bake for 20 minutes. Reduce the heat to 350°F and bake until the crust is golden and the filling is bubbling, about 15 more minutes.

Lemon Meringue Pie

Serve this by itself, hot, warm or cold. It doesn't need any accompaniment.

Serves 8

grated rind and juice of 1 large lemon

1 cup superfine sugar

2 tablespoons butter

3 tablespoons cornstarch

3 eggs, separated

pinch of salt

⅛ teaspoon cream of tartar

For the pastry

1 cup all-purpose flour

½ teaspoon salt

⅓ cup cold vegetable shortening, cut in pieces

1 For the pastry, sift the flour and salt into a bowl. Add the shortening and cut in with a pastry blender until the mixture resembles coarse crumbs. With a fork, stir in just enough ice water to bind the dough (about 2 tablespoons). Gather the dough into a ball.

2 On a lightly floured surface, roll out the dough ⅛ inch thick. Transfer to a 9-inch pie pan and trim the edge to leave a ½-inch overhang.

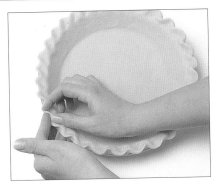

3 Fold the overhang under and crimp the edge. Chill the pie shell in the fridge for at least 20 minutes. Preheat the oven to 400°F.

4 Prick the dough all over with a fork. Line with waxed paper and fill with baking beans. Bake for 12 minutes. Remove the paper and beans and continue baking until golden, 6–8 minutes more.

5 In a saucepan, combine the lemon rind and juice, ½ cup of the sugar, the butter and 1 cup water. Bring the mixture to a boil.

6 Meanwhile, in a mixing bowl, dissolve the cornstarch in 1 tablespoon cold water. Add the egg yolks.

7 Add the egg yolks to the lemon mixture and return to a boil, whisking constantly, until the mixture thickens, about 5 minutes.

8 Cover the surface with waxed paper to prevent a skin from forming, and let cool.

9 For the meringue, beat the egg whites with the salt and cream of tartar using an electric mixer, until they hold stiff peaks. Add the remaining sugar and beat until glossy.

10 Spoon the lemon mixture into the pie shell and spread level. Spoon the meringue on top, smoothing it up to the edge of the crust to seal. Bake until golden, 12–15 minutes.

Chocolate Chiffon Pie

This light and creamy dessert is as luxurious as its name suggests.

Serves 8

6 ounces semisweet chocolate squares

1 ounce square unsweetened chocolate

1 cup milk

1 tablespoon gelatin

⅔ cup granulated sugar

2 jumbo eggs, separated

1 teaspoon vanilla extract

1½ cups whipping cream

pinch of salt

whipped cream and chocolate curls, to
   decorate

For the crust

1½ cups graham cracker crumbs

6 tablespoons butter, melted

1 Place a baking sheet in the oven and preheat to 350°F. For the crust, mix the graham cracker crumbs and butter in a bowl. Press the crumbs evenly over the bottom and sides of a 9-inch pie pan. Bake for 8 minutes. Let cool.

2 Chop the chocolate, then grind in a food processor or blender. Set aside.

3 Place the milk in the top of a double boiler or in a heatproof bowl. Sprinkle with the gelatin. Let stand 5 minutes to soften.

4 Set the top of the double boiler or heatproof bowl over hot water. Add ⅓ cup of the sugar, the chocolate and egg yolks. Stir until dissolved. Add the vanilla extract.

5 Set the top of the double boiler in a bowl of ice and stir until the mixture reaches room temperature. Remove from the ice and set aside.

6 Whip the cream lightly. Set aside. With an electric mixer, beat the egg whites and salt until soft peaks form. Add the remaining sugar and beat only enough to blend.

7 Fold a dollop of egg whites into the chocolate mixture, then pour back into the whites and gently fold in.

8 Fold in the whipped cream and pour into the pastry shell. Put in the freezer until just set, about 5 minutes. If the center sinks, fill with any remaining mixture. Chill for 3–4 hours. Decorate with whipped cream and chocolate curls. Serve cold.

Coconut Cream Pie

Once you have made the pastry, the delicious filling can be put together in moments.

INGREDIENTS

Serves 8

2½ cups shredded coconut

⅔ cup superfine sugar

¼ cup cornstarch

pinch of salt

2½ cups milk

¼ cup whipping cream

2 egg yolks

2 tablespoons unsalted butter

2 teaspoons vanilla extract

For the pastry

1 cup all-purpose flour

¼ teaspoon salt

3 tablespoons cold butter, cut in pieces

2 tablespoons cold vegetable shortening

1 For the pastry, sift the flour and salt into a bowl. Add the butter and shortening and cut in with a pastry blender or two knives until the mixture resembles coarse bread crumbs.

2 With a fork, stir in just enough ice water to bind the dough (2–3 tablespoons). Gather into a ball, wrap in waxed paper and chill for at least 20 minutes.

3 Preheat the oven to 425°F. Roll out the dough ⅛ inch thick. Transfer to a 9-inch tart pan. Trim and flute the edges. Prick the bottom. Line with waxed paper and fill with baking beans. Bake for 10–12 minutes. Remove the paper and beans, reduce the heat to 350°F and bake until brown, about 10–15 more minutes.

4 Spread 1 cup of the coconut on a baking sheet and toast in the oven until golden, 6–8 minutes, stirring often. Set aside for decorating.

5 Put the sugar, cornstarch and salt in a saucepan. In a bowl, whisk together the milk, cream and egg yolks. Add the egg mixture to the saucepan.

6 Cook over low heat, stirring constantly, until the mixture comes to a boil. Boil for 1 minute, then remove from the heat. Add the butter, vanilla extract and remaining coconut.

7 Pour into the pre-baked pastry shell. When the filling is cool, sprinkle toasted coconut in a ring in the center.

Peach Tart with Almond Cream

The almond cream filling should be baked until it is just turning brown. Take care not to over-bake it or the delicate flavors will be spoiled.

Serves 8–10

4 large ripe peaches

⅔ cup blanched almonds

2 tablespoons all-purpose flour

7 tablespoons unsalted butter, at room temperature

scant ¾ cup granulated sugar

1 egg

1 egg yolk

½ teaspoon vanilla extract, or 2 teaspoons rum

For the pastry

1¼ cups flour

¾ teaspoon salt

7 tablespoons cold unsalted butter, cut in pieces

1 egg yolk

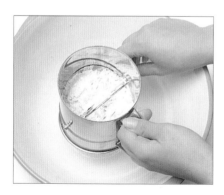

1 For the pastry, sift the flour and salt into a bowl.

2 Add the butter and cut in with a pastry blender until the mixture resembles coarse crumbs. With a fork, stir in the egg yolk and just enough ice water (2–3 tablespoons) to bind the dough. Gather into a ball, wrap in waxed paper and chill for at least 20 minutes. Place a baking sheet in the oven and preheat to 400°F.

3 On a lightly floured surface, roll out the pastry ⅛ inch thick. Transfer to a 10-inch tart pan. Trim the edge, prick the bottom and chill.

4 Score the bottoms of the peaches. Drop the peaches, one at a time, into boiling water. Leave for 20 seconds, then dip in cold water. Peel off the skins, using a sharp knife.

5 Grind the almonds finely with the flour in a food processor, blender or nut grinder. With an electric mixer, cream the butter and ½ cup of the sugar until light and fluffy. Gradually beat in the egg and yolk. Stir in the almonds and vanilla. Spread in the pastry shell.

6 Halve the peaches and remove the pits. Cut horizontally in thin slices and arrange on top of the almond cream like the spokes of a wheel; keep the slices of each peach half together. Fan them out by pressing down gently at a slight angle.

7 Bake until the pastry begins to brown, 10–15 minutes. Lower the heat to 350°F and continue baking until the almond cream sets, about 15 more minutes. Ten minutes before the end of the cooking time, sprinkle with the remaining sugar.

VARIATION

For a Nectarine and Apricot Tart with Almond Cream, replace the peaches with nectarines, prepared and arranged the same way. Peel and chop three fresh apricots. Fill the spaces between the fanned-out nectarines with chopped apricots. Bake as above.

Raspberry Tart

This glazed fruit tart really does taste as good as it looks.

Serves 8

4 egg yolks

⅓ cup granulated sugar

3 tablespoons all-purpose flour

1¼ cups milk

pinch of salt

½ teaspoon vanilla extract

3 cups fresh raspberries

5 tablespoons grape or red currant jelly

1 tablespoon fresh orange juice

For the pastry

1¼ cups all-purpose flour

½ teaspoon baking powder

¼ teaspoon salt

1 tablespoon sugar

grated rind of ½ orange

6 tablespoons cold butter, cut in pieces

1 egg yolk

3–4 tablespoons whipping cream

1 For the pastry, sift the flour, baking powder and salt into a bowl. Stir in the sugar and orange rind. Add the butter and mix until the mixture resembles coarse crumbs. With a fork, stir in the egg yolk and just enough cream to bind the dough. Gather into a ball, wrap in waxed paper and chill.

2 For the custard filling, beat the egg yolks and sugar until thick and lemon colored. Gradually stir in the flour.

3 In a saucepan, bring the milk and salt just to a boil, and remove from the heat. Whisk into the egg yolk mixture, return to the pan, and continue whisking over medium high heat until just bubbling. Cook for 3 minutes to thicken. Transfer immediately to a bowl. Stir in the vanilla to blend.

4 Cover with waxed paper to prevent a skin from forming.

5 Preheat the oven to 400°F. On a lightly floured surface, roll out the dough about ⅛ inch thick, transfer to a 10-inch tart pan and trim the edge. Prick the bottom all over with a fork and line with waxed paper. Fill with baking beans and bake for 15 minutes. Remove the paper and baking beans. Continue baking until golden, 6–8 minutes more. Let cool.

6 Spread an even layer of the pastry cream filling in the tart shell and arrange the raspberries on top. Melt the jelly and orange juice in a pan over low heat and brush on top to glaze.

Kiwi Ricotta Cheese Tart

It is well worth taking your time arranging the kiwi fruit topping in neat rows for this exotic and impressive-looking tart.

INGREDIENTS

Serves 8

½ cup blanched almonds

½ cup plus 1 tablespoon superfine sugar

4 cups ricotta cheese

1 cup whipping cream

1 egg

3 egg yolks

1 tablespoon all-purpose flour

pinch of salt

2 tablespoons rum

grated rind of 1 lemon

2½ tablespoons lemon juice

¼ cup honey

5 kiwi fruit

For the pastry

1¼ cups all-purpose flour

1 tablespoon granulated sugar

½ teaspoon salt

½ teaspoon baking powder

6 tablespoons cold butter, cut in pieces

1 egg yolk

3–4 tablespoons whipping cream

1 For the pastry, sift the flour, sugar, salt and baking powder into a bowl. Cut in the butter until the mixture resembles coarse crumbs. Mix the egg yolk and cream. Stir in just enough to bind the dough.

2 Transfer to a lightly floured surface, flatten slightly, wrap in waxed paper and chill for 30 minutes. Preheat the oven to 425°F.

3 On a lightly floured surface, roll out the dough ⅛ inch thick and transfer to a 9-inch spring-form pan. Crimp the edge.

4 Prick the bottom of the dough all over with a fork. Line with waxed paper and fill with baking beans. Bake for 10 minutes. Remove the paper and beans and bake until golden, 6–8 minutes more. Let cool. Reduce the heat to 350°F.

5 Grind the almonds finely with 1 tablespoon of the sugar in a food processor or blender.

6 With an electric mixer, beat the ricotta until creamy. Add the cream, egg, yolks, remaining sugar, flour, salt, rum, lemon rind and 2 tablespoons of the lemon juice. Beat to combine.

7 Stir in the ground almonds until well blended.

8 Pour into the shell and bake until golden, about 1 hour. Let cool, then chill, loosely covered, for 2–3 hours. Unmold and place on a serving plate.

9 Combine the honey and remaining lemon juice for the glaze. Set aside.

10 Peel the kiwis. Halve them lengthwise, then cut horizontally into ¼-inch slices. Arrange the slices in rows across the top of the tart. Just before serving, brush with the glaze.

Lemon and Orange Tart

Refreshing citrus fruits in a crisp, nutty pastry case.

INGREDIENTS

Serves 8–10

1 cup all-purpose flour, sifted

1 cup whole-wheat flour

3 tablespoons ground hazelnuts

3 tablespoons confectioners' sugar, sifted

pinch of salt

½ cup unsalted butter

¼ cup lemon curd

1¼ cups whipped cream or fromage frais

4 oranges, peeled and thinly sliced

1 Place the flours, hazelnuts, sugar, salt and butter in a food processor and process in short bursts until the mixture resembles bread crumbs. Add 2–3 tablespoons cold water and process until the dough comes together.

2 Turn out onto a lightly floured surface and knead gently until smooth. Roll out and line a 10-inch tart pan. Ease the pastry gently into the corners without stretching it. Chill for 20 minutes. Preheat the oven to 375°F.

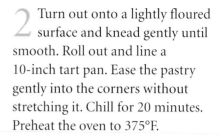

3 Line the pastry with waxed paper and fill with baking beans. Bake blind for 15 minutes, remove the paper and beans and continue for another 5–10 minutes, until the pastry is crisp. Let cool.

4 Whisk the lemon curd into the whipped cream and spread over the bottom of the pastry. Arrange the orange slices on top and serve at room temperature.

Chocolate Pear Tart

Serve slices of this drizzled with light cream or with a scoop of vanilla ice cream for a special treat.

Serves 8

4 ounces semisweet chocolate, grated

3 large firm ripe pears

1 egg

1 egg yolk

½ cup light cream or half-and-half

½ teaspoon vanilla extract

3 tablespoons superfine sugar

For the pastry

1 cup all-purpose flour

pinch of salt

2 tablespoons superfine sugar

½ cup cold unsalted butter, cut into pieces

1 egg yolk

1 tablespoon fresh lemon juice

1 For the pastry, sift the flour and salt into a bowl. Add the sugar and butter. Cut in with a pastry blender until the mixture resembles coarse crumbs. With a fork, stir in the egg yolk and lemon juice until the mixture forms a dough. Gather into a ball, wrap in waxed paper, and chill for at least 20 minutes.

2 Place a baking sheet in the oven and preheat to 400°F. On a lightly floured surface, roll out the dough to ⅛ inch thick and trim the edge. Transfer to a 10-inch tart pan.

3 Sprinkle the bottom of the tart shell with the grated chocolate.

4 Peel, halve and core the pears. Cut in thin slices horizontally, then fan them out slightly.

5 Transfer the pear halves to the tart with the help of a metal spatula and arrange on top of the chocolate to resemble the spokes of a wheel.

6 Whisk together the egg and egg yolk, cream and vanilla extract. Ladle over the pears, then sprinkle with sugar.

7 Bake for 10 minutes. Reduce the heat to 350°F and cook until the custard is set and the pears begin to caramelize, about 20 more minutes. Serve at room temperature.

Blueberry-Hazelnut Cheesecake

The shell for this cheesecake is made with ground hazelnuts – a tasty and unusual alternative to a cookie crust.

INGREDIENTS

Serves 6–8

12 ounces blueberries

1 tablespoon honey

6 tablespoons granulated sugar

juice of 1 lemon

¾ cup cream cheese, at room temperature

1 egg

1 teaspoon hazelnut liqueur (optional)

½ cup whipping cream

For the base

1⅔ cups ground hazelnuts

⅔ cup all-purpose flour

pinch of salt

¼ cup butter, at room temperature

⅓ cup light brown sugar, firmly packed

1 egg yolk

1 For the shell, put the hazelnuts in a large bowl. Sift in the flour and salt, and stir to mix. Set aside.

2 Beat the butter with the brown sugar until light and fluffy. Beat in the egg yolk. Gradually fold in the nut mixture, in three batches, until well combined.

3 Press the dough into a greased 9-inch pie pan, spreading it evenly against the sides. Form a rim around the top edge that is slightly thicker than the sides. Cover and chill for at least 30 minutes.

4 Preheat the oven to 350°F. Meanwhile, for the topping, combine the blueberries, honey, 1 tablespoon of the granulated sugar and 1 teaspoon lemon juice in a heavy saucepan. Cook the mixture over low heat, stirring occasionally, until the berries have given off some liquid but still retain their shape, 5–7 minutes. Remove from the heat and set aside.

5 Place the pastry shell in the oven and bake for 15 minutes. Remove and let cool while making the filling.

6 Beat together the cream cheese and remaining granulated sugar until light and fluffy. Add the egg, 1 tablespoon lemon juice, the liqueur, if using, and the cream, and beat until thoroughly blended.

7 Pour the cheese mixture into the pastry shell and spread evenly. Bake until just set, 20–25 minutes.

8 Let the cheesecake cool completely on a wire rack, then cover and chill for at least 1 hour.

9 Spread the blueberry mixture evenly over the top of the cheesecake. Serve at room temperature.

COOK'S TIP

The cheesecake can be prepared 1 day in advance, but add the fruit shortly before serving.

Raspberry and White Chocolate Cheesecake

Raspberries and white chocolate are an irresistible combination, especially when teamed with rich mascarpone on a crunchy ginger and pecan base.

INGREDIENTS

Serves 8

¼ cup unsalted butter

2⅓ cups ginger cookies, crushed

½ cup chopped pecans or walnuts

For the filling

1¼ cups mascarpone

¾ cup fromage frais or cream cheese

2 eggs, beaten

3 tablespoons superfine sugar

9 ounces white chocolate, broken into squares

1⅓ cups fresh or thawed frozen raspberries

For the topping

½ cup mascarpone

⅓ cup fromage frais or cream cheese

white chocolate curls and raspberries, to decorate

1 Preheat the oven to 300°F. Melt the butter in a saucepan, then stir in the crushed cookies and nuts. Press into the bottom of a 9-inch springform cake pan.

2 Make the filling. Beat the mascarpone and fromage frais in a bowl, then beat in the eggs and superfine sugar until evenly mixed.

3 Melt the white chocolate gently in a heatproof bowl over hot water.

4 Stir the chocolate into the cheese mixture with the raspberries.

5 Transfer to the prepared pan and spread evenly, then bake for about 1 hour or until just set. Turn off the oven, but do not remove the cheesecake. Leave it until cold and completely set.

6 Release the pan and lift the cheesecake onto a plate. Make the topping by mixing the mascarpone and fromage frais in a bowl and spread over the cheesecake. Decorate with chocolate curls and raspberries.

Sticky Tart

This British favorite is filling, so serve after a light meal.

INGREDIENTS

Serves 4–6

¾ cup light corn syrup

1½ cups fresh white bread crumbs

grated rind of 1 lemon

2 tablespoons fresh lemon juice

For the pastry

1¼ cups flour

½ teaspoon salt

6 tablespoons cold unsalted butter, cut in pieces

3 tablespoons cold margarine, cut in pieces

1 For the pastry, combine the flour and salt in a bowl. Add the butter and margarine and cut in with a pastry blender until the mixture resembles coarse crumbs.

2 With a fork, stir in just enough ice water (about 3–4 tablespoons) to bind the dough. Gather into a ball, wrap in waxed paper, and chill for at least 20 minutes.

3 On a lightly floured surface, roll out the dough ⅛ inch thick. Transfer to an 8-inch tart pan and trim off the overhang. Chill for at least 20 minutes. Reserve the trimmings for the lattice top.

4 Place a baking sheet above the center of the oven and heat to 400°F.

5 In a saucepan, warm the syrup until thin and runny.

6 Remove from the heat and stir in the bread crumbs and lemon rind. Let sit for 10 minutes so the bread can absorb the syrup. Add more bread crumbs if the mixture is thin. Stir in the lemon juice and spread evenly in the pastry shell.

7 Roll out the pastry trimmings and cut into 10–12 thin strips.

8 Lay half the strips on the filling, then carefully arrange the remaining strips to form a lattice pattern.

9 Place on the hot sheet and bake for 10 minutes. Lower the heat to 375°F. Bake until golden, about 15 minutes more. Serve warm or cold.

Rich Chocolate-Berry Tart

Use any berries you like to top this exotic tart.

INGREDIENTS

Serves 10

½ cup unsalted butter, softened

½ cup superfine sugar

½ teaspoon salt

1 tablespoon vanilla extract

½ cup unsweetened cocoa

1¾ cups all-purpose flour

1 pound fresh berries for topping

For the chocolate ganache filling

2 cups heavy cream

½ cup seedless blackberry preserves

8 ounces semisweet chocolate, chopped

2 tablespoons unsalted butter

For the blackberry sauce

8 ounces fresh or frozen blackberries
or raspberries

1 tablespoon lemon juice

2 tablespoons superfine sugar

2 tablespoons blackberry liqueur

1 Prepare the pastry. Place the butter, sugar, salt and vanilla in a food processor and process until creamy. Add the cocoa and process for 1 minute. Add the flour all at once and process for 10–15 seconds, until just blended. Place a piece of plastic wrap on the work surface. Turn out the dough onto the plastic wrap. Use the wrap to help shape the dough into a flat circle and wrap tightly. Chill for 1 hour.

2 Lightly grease a 9-inch tart pan with a removable bottom. Roll out the dough between two sheets of plastic wrap to an 11-inch round, about ¼ inch thick. Peel off the top sheet of plastic wrap and invert the dough into the prepared pan. Ease the dough into the pan. Remove the plastic wrap.

3 With floured fingers, press the dough onto the bottom and sides of the pan, then roll a rolling pin over the edge of the pan to cut off any excess dough. Prick the dough with a fork. Chill for 1 hour. Preheat the oven to 350°F. Line the tart with foil or baking paper; fill with dry beans. Bake for 10 minutes; lift out the foil with the beans and bake for 5 more minutes, until just set (pastry may look underdone on the bottom, but will dry out). Remove to a wire rack to cool.

4 Prepare the filling. In a medium saucepan over medium heat, bring the cream and blackberry preserves to a boil. Remove from the heat and add the chocolate, stirring until smooth. Stir in the butter and strain into the cooled tart, smoothing the top. Cool the tart completely.

5 Prepare the sauce. In a food processor combine the blackberries, lemon juice and sugar and process until smooth. Strain into a bowl and add the liqueur. If it is too thick, thin with a little water.

6 To serve, remove the tart from the pan. Place on a serving plate and arrange the berries on top. With a pastry brush, brush the berries with a little of the blackberry sauce to glaze lightly. Serve the remaining sauce separately.

Almond Custard

Although the pastry shell makes this a tart, the original recipe describes it as a pudding.

INGREDIENTS

Serves 4

8 ounces puff pastry

2 tablespoons raspberry or apricot jam

2 eggs

2 egg yolks

generous ½ cup superfine sugar

½ cup butter, melted

½ cup ground almonds

few drops of almond extract

confectioners' sugar, for sifting

1 Preheat the oven to 400°F. Roll out the pastry on a lightly floured surface and use it to line a 7-inch pie plate or loose-bottomed tart pan. Spread the jam over the bottom of the pastry shell.

COOK'S TIP

Since this pastry shell isn't baked blind first, place a baking sheet in the oven while it preheats, then place the tart pan on the hot sheet. This will ensure that the bottom of the pastry shell is cooked all the way through.

2 Whisk the eggs, egg yolks and sugar together in a large bowl until thick and pale.

3 Gently stir the butter, ground almonds and almond extract into the mixture.

4 Pour the mixture into the pastry shell and bake for 30 minutes, until the filling is just set and browned. Sift confectioners' sugar over the top before serving the tart hot, warm or cold.

VARIATION

Ground hazelnuts are increasingly available and make an interesting change to the almonds in this tart. If you are going to grind shelled hazelnuts yourself, first roast them in the oven for 10–15 minutes to bring out their flavor, then rub in a dishtowel to remove skins.

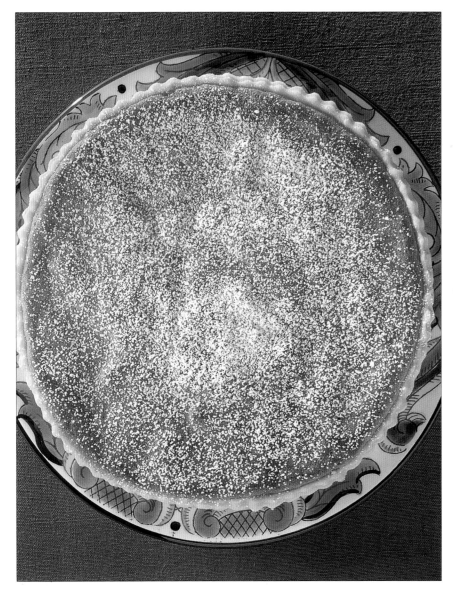

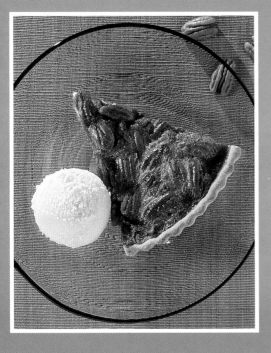

INTERNATIONAL
CLASSICS

Apple Pie

Delicious on its own or with a dollop of heavy cream or ice cream.

Serves 8

2 pounds tart apples

2 tablespoons all-purpose flour

½ cup sugar

1½ tablespoons fresh lemon juice

½ teaspoon ground cinnamon

½ teaspoon ground allspice

¼ teaspoon ground ginger

¼ teaspoon grated nutmeg

¼ teaspoon salt

¼ cup unsalted butter, diced

For the pastry

2 cups all-purpose flour

1 teaspoon salt

6 tablespoons cold butter, cut in pieces

¼ cup cold vegetable shortening, cut in
   pieces

1 For the pastry, sift the flour and salt into a bowl.

2 Add the butter and shortening and cut in with a pastry blender or rub between your fingertips until the mixture resembles coarse crumbs. With a fork, stir in just enough ice water to bind the dough (4–8 tablespoons).

3 Gather into two balls, wrap in waxed paper and chill for 20 minutes.

4 On a lightly floured surface, roll out one dough ball to ⅛ inch thick. Transfer to a 9-inch pie pan and trim the edge. Place a baking sheet in the center of the oven and preheat to 425°F.

5 Peel, core and slice the apples into a bowl. Toss with the flour, sugar, lemon juice, spices and salt. Spoon into the pie shell and dot with butter.

6 Roll out the remaining dough. Place on top of the pie and trim to leave a ¾-inch overhang. Fold the overhang under the bottom dough and press to seal. Crimp the edge.

7 Roll out the scraps and cut out leaf shapes and roll balls for the holly decoration. Arrange on top of the pie. Cut steam vents.

8 Bake for 10 minutes. Reduce the heat to 350°F and bake until golden, 40–45 more minutes. If the pie browns too quickly, protect with foil.

Apple Brown Betty

This simple dessert tastes good with cream or ice cream.

Serves 6

1 cup fresh bread crumbs

¾ cup light brown sugar, firmly packed

½ teaspoon ground cinnamon

¼ teaspoon ground cloves

¼ teaspoon grated nutmeg

¼ cup butter

2 pounds tart-sweet apples

juice of 1 lemon

⅓ cup finely chopped walnuts

1 Preheat the broiler. Spread the bread crumbs on a baking sheet and toast under the broiler until golden, stirring so they color evenly. Set aside.

2 Preheat the oven to 375°F. Butter a 2-quart baking dish. Set aside.

3 Mix the sugar with the spices. Cut the butter into pea-size pieces. Set aside.

4 Peel, core and slice the apples. Toss immediately with the lemon juice to prevent the apple slices from turning brown.

5 Sprinkle about 2½ tablespoons of the bread crumbs over the bottom of the prepared dish. Cover with a third of the apple slices and sprinkle with a third of the sugar-spice mixture. Add another layer of bread crumbs and dot with a third of the butter. Repeat the layers two more times, ending with a layer of bread crumbs. Sprinkle with the nuts, and dot with the remaining butter.

6 Bake until the apples are tender and the top is golden brown, 35–40 minutes. Serve warm or cold.

Spiced Pumpkin Pie

An unofficial national dish, appearing in full glory at Thanksgiving.

INGREDIENTS

Serves 4–6

1½ cups all-purpose flour

pinch of salt

6 tablespoons unsalted butter

1 tablespoon superfine sugar

4 cups peeled fresh pumpkin, cubed, or
    2 cups canned pumpkin, drained

½ cup light brown sugar

¼ teaspoon salt

¼ teaspoon ground allspice

½ teaspoon ground cinnamon

½ teaspoon ground ginger

2 eggs, lightly beaten

½ cup heavy cream

whipped cream, to serve

1 Place the flour in a bowl with the salt and butter and rub with your fingertips until the mixture resembles bread crumbs (or use a food processor).

2 Stir in the sugar and add about 2–3 tablespoons water and mix to a soft dough. Knead the dough lightly on a floured surface. Flatten out into a round, wrap in a plastic bag and chill for 1 hour.

3 Preheat the oven to 400°F with a baking sheet inside. If you are using raw pumpkin for the pie, steam for 15 minutes until quite tender, then let cool completely. Purée the steamed or canned pumpkin in a food processor or blender until it is very smooth.

4 Roll out the pastry quite thinly and use to line a 9-inch (measured across the top) deep pie pan. Trim off any excess pastry and reserve for the decoration. Prick the base of the pastry shell with a fork.

5 Cut as many leaf shapes as you can from the excess pastry and make vein markings with the back of a knife on each. Brush the edge of the pastry with water and stick the leaves all around the edge. Chill.

6 In a large bowl combine the pumpkin purée, sugar, salt, spices, eggs and cream and pour into the prepared pastry shell. Smooth the top with a knife.

7 Place on the preheated baking sheet and bake for 15 minutes. Then reduce the temperature to 350°F and cook for another 30 minutes, or until the filling is set and the pastry golden. Serve the pie warm with a generous dollop of whipped cream.

Classic Cheesecake

You can decorate this with fruit and serve it with cream, if desired, but it tastes delicious just as it is.

INGREDIENTS

Serves 8

½ cup graham cracker crumbs

2 pounds cream cheese

1¼ cups superfine sugar

grated rind of 1 lemon

3 tablespoons fresh lemon juice

1 teaspoon vanilla extract

4 eggs, at room temperature

1 Preheat the oven to 325°F. Grease a 9-inch springform cake pan. Place on a round of foil 5 inches larger than the diameter of the pan. Press it up the sides to seal tightly.

2 Sprinkle the crumbs in the bottom of the pan. Press to form an even layer.

3 With an electric mixer, beat the cream cheese until smooth. Add the sugar, lemon rind and juice and vanilla extract, and beat until blended. Beat in the eggs, one at a time. Beat just enough to blend thoroughly.

4 Pour into the prepared pan. Set the pan in a larger baking tray and place in the oven. Pour enough hot water in the outer tray to come 1 inch up the side of the pan.

5 Bake until the top of the cake is golden brown, about 1½ hours. Let cool in the pan.

6 Run a knife around the edge to loosen, then remove the rim of the pan. Chill for at least 4 hours before serving.

Chocolate Cheesecake

This popular variation of the classic dessert is made with a cinnamon and chocolate base.

INGREDIENTS

Serves 10–12

6 ounces semisweet chocolate squares

4 ounces bitter chocolate squares

2½ pounds cream cheese, at room temperature

1 cup superfine sugar

2 teaspoons vanilla extract

4 eggs, at room temperature

¾ cup sour cream

For the base

1½ cups chocolate wafer crumbs

6 tablespoons butter, melted

½ teaspoon ground cinnamon

1 Preheat the oven to 350°F. Grease a 9-inch springform cake pan.

2 For the shell, mix the chocolate wafer crumbs with the butter and cinnamon. Press evenly in the bottom of the pan.

3 Melt the semisweet and bitter chocolate in the top of a heavy boiler, or in a heatproof bowl set over hot water. Set aside.

4 With an electric mixer, beat the cream cheese until smooth, then beat in the sugar and vanilla extract. Add the eggs, one at a time, scraping the bowl with a spatula when necessary.

5 Add the sour cream. Stir in the melted chocolate.

6 Pour into the pan. Bake for 1 hour. Let cool in the pan; remove rim. Chill before serving.

Mississippi Pecan Pie

This fabulous dessert is an American original but has become an international favorite.

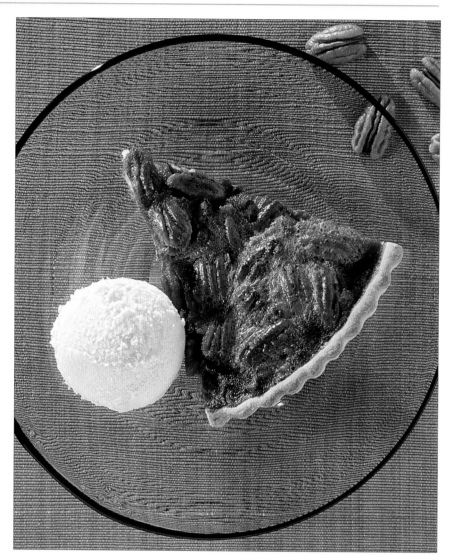

INGREDIENTS

Serves 6–8

For the pastry

1 cup all-purpose flour

¼ cup butter, cubed

2 tablespoons superfine sugar

1 egg yolk

For the filling

½ cup light corn syrup

⅓ cup dark brown sugar

¼ cup butter

3 eggs, lightly beaten

½ teaspoon vanilla extract

1¼ cups pecans

fresh cream or ice cream, to serve

1 Place the flour in a bowl and add the butter. Rub in the butter with your fingertips until the mixture resembles bread crumbs, then stir in the sugar, egg yolk and about 2 tablespoons cold water. Mix to a dough and knead lightly on a floured surface until smooth.

2 Roll out the pastry and use to line an 8-inch loose-bottomed fluted tart pan. Prick the bottom, then line with waxed paper and fill with baking beans. Chill for 30 minutes. Preheat the oven to 400°F.

3 Bake the pastry shell for 10 minutes. Remove the paper and beans and bake for 5 minutes. Reduce the oven temperature to 350°F.

4 Meanwhile, heat the syrup, sugar and butter in a pan until the sugar dissolves. Remove from the heat and cool slightly. Whisk in the eggs and vanilla extract and stir in the pecans.

5 Pour into the pastry shell and bake for 35–40 minutes, until the filling is set. Serve with cream or ice cream.

Boston Banoffee Pie

There are many variations of this treat; this one is easy to make and tastes wonderful.

INGREDIENTS

Serves 6–8

1¼ cups all-purpose flour

1 cup butter

¼ cup superfine sugar

1 can (14 ounces) low-fat, sweetened condensed milk

⅔ cup light brown sugar

2 tablespoons light corn syrup

2 small bananas, sliced

a little lemon juice

whipped cream, to decorate

1 teaspoon grated semisweet chocolate

1 Preheat the oven to 325°F. Place the flour and ½ cup of the butter in a food processor and blend until crumbed (or rub in with your fingertips). Stir in the superfine sugar.

2 Squeeze the mixture together until it forms a dough. Press into the bottom of an 8-inch loose-bottomed fluted tart pan. Bake for 25–30 minutes.

3 Place the remaining butter with the condensed milk, brown sugar and corn syrup in a large nonstick saucepan and heat gently, stirring, until the butter has melted and the sugar has dissolved.

4 Bring to a gentle boil and cook for 7 minutes, stirring constantly (to prevent burning), until the mixture thickens and turns a light caramel color. Pour onto the cooked pastry shell and let stand until cold.

5 Sprinkle the bananas with the lemon juice and arrange in overlapping circles on top of the caramel filling, leaving a gap in the center. Pipe a swirl of whipped cream in the center and sprinkle with the grated chocolate.

Vermont Baked Maple Custard

Try to find pure maple syrup for this custard as it will really enhance the flavor.

INGREDIENTS

Serves 6

3 eggs

½ cup pure maple syrup

2½ cups milk

pinch of salt

pinch of grated nutmeg

COOK'S TIP

Baking delicate mixtures such as custards in a water bath helps protect them from uneven heating that could make them rubbery.

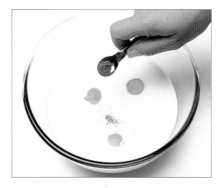

1 Preheat the oven to 350°F. Combine all the ingredients in a large bowl and mix thoroughly.

2 Set individual custard cups or ramekins in a roasting pan half filled with hot water. Pour the custard mixture into the cups. Bake until the custards are set, 45 minutes to 1 hour. Test by inserting the blade of a knife in the center: It should come out clean. Serve warm or chilled.

Crème Caramel

Crème caramel is one of the most popular French desserts and is wonderful when freshly made. This is a slightly lighter modern version of the traditional recipe.

INGREDIENTS

Serves 6–8

1¼ cups granulated sugar

¼ cup water

1 vanilla bean or 2 teaspoons vanilla extract

1⅔ cups milk

1 cup whipping cream

5 large eggs

2 egg yolks

1 Put 1 cup of the sugar in a small heavy saucepan with ¼ cup of water to moisten. Bring to a boil over high heat, swirling the pan to dissolve the sugar. Boil, without stirring, until the syrup turns a dark caramel color (this will take about 4–5 minutes).

2 Immediately pour the caramel into a 4-cup soufflé dish. Holding the dish with oven gloves, quickly swirl the dish to coat the base and sides with the caramel and set aside. (The caramel will harden quickly as it cools.) Place the dish in a small roasting pan.

3 Preheat the oven to 325°F. With a small, sharp knife, carefully split the vanilla bean lengthwise and scrape the black seeds into a medium saucepan or add the vanilla extract. Add the milk and cream and bring just to a boil over medium-high heat, stirring frequently. Remove the pan from the heat, cover and set aside for 15–20 minutes.

4 In a bowl, whisk the eggs and egg yolks with the remaining sugar for 2–3 minutes, until smooth and creamy. Whisk in the hot milk and carefully strain the mixture into the caramel-lined dish. Cover with foil.

5 Place the dish in a roasting pan and pour in enough boiling water to come halfway up the sides of the dish. Bake the custard for 40–45 minutes, until just set and a knife inserted about 2 inches from the edge comes out clean. Remove from the roasting pan and cool for at least 30 minutes, then chill overnight.

6 To turn out, carefully run a sharp knife around the edge of the dish to loosen the custard. Cover the dish with a serving plate and, holding them tightly, invert the dish and plate together. Gently lift one edge of the dish, letting the caramel run over the sides, then slowly lift off the dish.

Apple Strudel

This Austrian pudding is traditionally made with paper-thin layers of buttered strudel pastry, filled with spiced apples and nuts. Ready-made filo pastry makes an easy substitute.

Serves 4–6

¾ cup hazelnuts, chopped and roasted

2 tablespoons slivered almonds, roasted

¼ cup raw sugar

½ teaspoon ground cinnamon

grated rind and juice of ½ lemon

2 large Bramley apples, peeled, cored
    and chopped

⅓ cup golden raisins

4 large sheets filo pastry

¼ cup unsalted butter, melted

confectioners' sugar, for dusting

cream, custard or yogurt, to serve

1 Preheat the oven to 375°F. In a bowl combine the hazelnuts, almonds, sugar, cinnamon, lemon rind and juice, apples and golden raisins. Set aside.

2 Lay one sheet of filo pastry on a clean dishtowel and brush with melted butter. Lay a second sheet on top and brush again with melted butter. Repeat with the remaining two sheets.

3 Spread the fruit and nut mixture over the pastry, leaving a 3-inch border at the shorter ends. Fold the ends in over the filling. Roll up from one long edge, using the dishtowel.

4 Transfer the strudel to a greased baking sheet, placing it seam side down. Brush with butter and bake for 30–35 minutes, until golden and crisp. Dust with confectioners' sugar and serve hot with cream, custard or yogurt.

Chocolate Fruit Fondue

Fondues originated in Switzerland and this sweet treat is the perfect ending to any meal.

Serves 6–8

16 fresh strawberries

4 rings fresh pineapple, cut into wedges

2 small nectarines, pitted and cut
    into wedges

1 kiwi fruit, halved and thickly sliced

small bunch of black seedless grapes

2 bananas, chopped

1 small eating apple, cored and cut
    into wedges

lemon juice, for brushing

8 ounces semisweet chocolate

1 tablespoon butter

⅔ cup light cream or half-and-half

3 tablespoons Irish cream liqueur

1 tablespoon pistachios, chopped

1 Arrange the fruit on a serving platter and brush the banana and apple pieces with a little lemon juice. Cover and place in the fridge until ready to serve.

2 Place the chocolate, butter, cream and liqueur in a bowl over a pan of simmering water. Stir until melted and completely smooth.

3 Pour the mixture into a warmed serving bowl; sprinkle with pistachios. Guests help themselves by skewering fruits onto forks and dipping in the hot sauce.

Floating Islands

Originally these oval-shaped meringues were poached in milk and this was then used to make the rich custard sauce.

INGREDIENTS

Serves 4–6

1 vanilla bean

2½ cups milk

8 egg yolks

¼ cup granulated sugar

For the meringues

4 jumbo egg whites

¼ teaspoon cream of tartar

1¼ cups superfine sugar

For the caramel

¾ cup granulated sugar

1 Split the vanilla bean lengthwise and scrape the seeds into a saucepan. Add the milk and bring just to a boil over medium heat, stirring frequently. Cover and set aside for 15–20 minutes.

2 In a medium bowl, whisk the egg yolks and sugar for 2–3 minutes, until thick and creamy. Whisk in the hot milk and return the mixture to the saucepan. With a wooden spoon, stir over medium-low heat until the sauce begins to thicken and coat the back of the spoon (do not let boil). Immediately strain into a chilled bowl, let cool, stirring occasionally, and then chill.

3 Half-fill a large wide frying pan or saucepan with water and bring just to the simmering point. In a clean, grease-free bowl, whisk the egg whites until frothy. Add the cream of tartar and continue whisking until they form soft peaks. Sprinkle over the superfine sugar, about 2 table-spoons at a time, and whisk until the whites are stiff and glossy.

4 Using two tablespoons, form egg-shaped meringues and slide them into the water (you may need to work in batches). Poach them for 2–3 minutes, turning once until just firm. Using a large slotted spoon, transfer the cooked meringues to a baking sheet lined with paper towels to drain.

5 Pour the cold custard into individual serving dishes and arrange the meringues on top.

6 To make the caramel, put the sugar into a small saucepan with 3 tablespoons water to moisten. Bring to a boil over high heat, swirling the pan to dissolve the sugar. Boil, without stirring, until the syrup turns a dark caramel color. Immediately drizzle the caramel over the meringues and custard in a zigzag pattern. Serve cold. (The caramel will soften if made too far ahead.)

Crème Brûlée

This dessert actually originated in England, but has become associated with France and is widely eaten there. Add a little liqueur, if desired, but it is equally delicious without it.

INGREDIENTS

Serves 6

1 vanilla bean

4 cups heavy cream

6 egg yolks

½ cup superfine sugar

2 tablespoons almond or orange liqueur
  (optional)

⅓ cup light brown sugar

1 Preheat the oven to 300°F. Place six ½-cup ramekins in a roasting pan and set aside.

2 With a small, sharp knife, split the vanilla bean lengthwise and scrape the black seeds into a medium saucepan. Add the cream and bring just to a boil over medium heat, stirring. Remove from the heat and cover. Set aside for 15–20 minutes.

3 In a bowl, whisk the egg yolks, superfine sugar and liqueur, if using, until well blended. Whisk in the hot cream and strain into a large pitcher. Divide the custard equally among the ramekins.

4 Pour enough boiling water into the roasting pan to come halfway up the sides of the ramekins. Cover the pan with foil and bake for about 30 minutes, until the custards are just set. Remove from the pan and let cool. Return to the dry roasting pan and chill.

5 Preheat the broiler. Sprinkle the sugar evenly over the surface of each custard and broiler for 30–60 seconds until the sugar melts and caramelizes. (Do not let the sugar burn or the custard curdle.) Place in the fridge to set the crust and chill completely before serving.

COOK'S TIP

To test if the custards are ready, push the point of a knife into center of one – if it comes out clean, the custards are cooked.

Crêpes Suzette

This is one of the best-known French desserts and is easy to make at home. You can make the crêpes in advance, then you will be able to put the dish together quickly at the last minute.

Serves 6

1 cup all-purpose flour

¼ teaspoon salt

2 tablespoons superfine sugar

2 eggs, lightly beaten

1 cup milk

2 tablespoons orange flower water or
    orange liqueur (optional)

2 tablespoons unsalted butter, melted,
    plus more for frying

For the orange sauce

6 tablespoons unsalted butter

¼ cup superfine sugar

grated rind and juice of 1 large
    unwaxed orange

grated rind and juice of 1 unwaxed lemon

⅔ cup fresh orange juice

¼ cup orange liqueur, plus more for
    flaming (optional)

brandy, for flaming (optional)

orange segments, to decorate

1 In a medium bowl, sift together the flour, salt and sugar. Make a well in the center and pour in the beaten eggs. Using a whisk, beat the eggs, bringing in a little flour until it is all incorporated. Slowly whisk in the milk and ¼ cup water to make a smooth batter.

2 Whisk in the orange flower water, if using, then strain the batter into a pitcher and set aside for 20–30 minutes. If the batter thickens, add a little milk or water to thin.

3 Heat a 7–8-inch crêpe pan over medium heat. Stir the melted butter into the crêpe batter. Brush the hot pan with a little extra melted butter and pour in about 2 tablespoons of batter. Quickly tilt and rotate the pan to cover the bottom with a thin layer of batter. Cook for about 1 minute, until the top is set and the bottom is golden. With a spatula, carefully turn over the crêpe and cook for 20–30 seconds, just to set. Turn out onto a plate.

4 Continue cooking the crêpes, stirring the batter occasionally and brushing the pan with a little melted butter when necessary. Place a sheet of plastic wrap between each crêpe as they are stacked to prevent sticking.

5 To make the sauce, melt the butter in a large frying pan over medium-low heat, then stir in the sugar, orange and lemon rind and juice, the additional orange juice and the orange liqueur, if using.

6 Place a crêpe in the pan, golden side down, swirling gently to coat with the sauce. Fold it in half, then in half again to form a triangle and push to the side of the pan. Continue heating and folding the crêpes until all are warm and covered with the sauce.

7 To flame the crêpes, heat 2–3 tablespoons each of orange liqueur and brandy in a small saucepan over medium heat. Remove the pan from the heat, carefully ignite the liquid with a match, then gently pour it over the crêpes. Scatter the orange segments over the crêpes and serve immediately.

Tarte au Citron

You can find this classic lemon tart in bistros all over France.

Serves 8–10

12 ounces pie or sweet pie pastry

grated rind of 2 or 3 lemons

⅔ cup freshly squeezed lemon juice

½ cup superfine sugar

¼ cup crème fraîche or heavy cream

4 eggs, plus 3 egg yolks

confectioners' sugar, for dusting

1 Preheat the oven to 375°F. Roll out the pastry thinly and use to line a 9-inch tart pan. Prick the bottom of the pastry.

2 Line the pastry shell with foil and fill with baking beans. Bake for about 15 minutes, until the edges are set and dry. Remove the foil and beans and continue baking for another 5–7 minutes, until golden.

3 Place the lemon rind, juice and sugar in a bowl. Beat until combined and then gradually add the crème fraîche and beat until well blended.

4 Beat in the eggs, one at a time, then beat in the egg yolks and pour the filling into the pastry shell. Bake for 15–20 minutes, until the filling is set. If the pastry begins to brown too much, cover the edges with foil. Let cool. Dust with a little confectioners' sugar before serving.

Pear and Almond Cream Tart

This tart is equally successful made with other kinds of fruit, and some variation can be seen in almost every good French pâtisserie. Try making it with nectarines, peaches, apricots or apples.

INGREDIENTS

Serves 6

12 ounces pie or sweet pie pastry

3 firm pears

lemon juice

1 tablespoon peach brandy or water

¼ cup peach preserve, strained

For the almond cream filling

¾ cup blanched whole almonds

¼ cup superfine sugar

5 tablespoons butter

1 egg, plus 1 egg white

few drops almond extract

1 Roll out the pastry thinly and use to line a 9-inch tart pan. Chill the pastry shell while you make the filling. Put the almonds and sugar in a food processor and pulse until finely ground; they should not be pasty. Add the butter and process until creamy, then add the egg, egg white and almond extract and mix well.

2 Place a baking sheet in the oven and preheat to 375°F. Peel the pears, halve them, remove the cores and rub with lemon juice.

3 Put the pear halves cut-side down on a board and slice thinly horizontally, keeping the slices together.

4 Pour the almond cream filling into the pastry shell. Slide a spatula under one pear half and press the top with your fingers to fan out the slices. Transfer to the tart, placing the fruit on the filling like spokes of a wheel. If desired, remove a few slices from each half before arranging and use to fill in any gaps in the center.

5 Place on the baking sheet and bake for 50–55 minutes, until the filling is set and browned. Cool on a rack.

6 Meanwhile, heat the brandy and the preserve in a small saucepan, then brush over the top of the hot tart to glaze. Serve the tart warm or at room temperature.

Sachertorte

This glorious torte was created in Vienna in 1832 by Franz Sacher, a chef in the royal household.

Serves 10–12

8 ounces semisweet dark chocolate,
   broken into squares
⅔ cup unsalted butter, softened
generous ½ cup superfine sugar
8 eggs, separated
1 cup all-purpose flour

For the glaze
scant 1 cup apricot jam
1 tablespoon lemon juice

For the icing
8 ounces semisweet dark chocolate,
   broken into squares
1 cup superfine sugar
1 tablespoon light corn syrup
1 cup heavy cream
1 teaspoon vanilla extract
plain chocolate curls, to decorate

1 Preheat the oven to 350°F. Grease a 9-inch round spring-form cake pan and line with waxed paper. Melt the chocolate in a heatproof bowl over hot water, then remove from the heat.

2 Cream the butter with the sugar in a mixing bowl until pale and fluffy, then add the egg yolks, one at a time, beating after each addition. Beat in the melted chocolate, then sift the flour over the mixture and fold it in evenly.

3 Whisk the egg whites in a clean, grease-free bowl until stiff, then stir about a quarter of the whites into the chocolate mixture to lighten it. Fold in the remaining whites.

4 Transfer the mixture to the prepared cake pan and smooth level. Bake for about 50–55 minutes or until firm. Turn out onto a wire rack to cool.

5 Heat the apricot jam with the lemon juice in a small saucepan until melted, then strain through a sieve into a bowl. Once the cake is cold, slice in half horizontally to make two equal-size layers.

6 Brush the top and sides of each layer with the apricot glaze, then sandwich them together. Place on a wire rack.

7 Mix the icing ingredients in a heavy saucepan. Heat gently, stirring until thick. Simmer for 3–4 minutes, without stirring, until the mixture registers 200°F on a sugar thermometer. Pour quickly over the cake and spread evenly. Let set, then decorate with chocolate curls.

Chocolate Soufflés

These are easy to make and can be prepared in advance – the filled dishes can wait for up to one hour before baking. For best results, use good quality Continental chocolate.

INGREDIENTS

Serves 6

6 ounces semisweet chocolate, chopped

⅔ cup unsalted butter, cut in small pieces

4 large eggs, separated

2 tablespoons orange liqueur (optional)

¼ teaspoon cream of tartar

3 tablespoons superfine sugar

confectioners' sugar, for dusting

sprigs of red currants and white chocolate roses, to decorate

For the white chocolate sauce

3 ounces white chocolate, chopped

6 tablespoons whipping cream

1–2 tablespoons orange liqueur

grated rind of ½ orange

1 Generously butter six small ramekins. Sprinkle each with a little superfine sugar and tap out any excess. Place the ramekins on a baking sheet.

2 In a heavy saucepan over very low heat, melt the chocolate and butter, stirring until smooth. Remove from the heat and cool slightly, then beat in the egg yolks and orange liqueur, if using. Set aside, stirring occasionally.

3 Preheat the oven to 425°F. In a clean, grease-free bowl, whisk the egg whites slowly until frothy. Add the cream of tartar, increase the speed and whisk until they form soft peaks. Gradually sprinkle on the sugar, 1 tablespoon at a time, whisking until the whites are stiff and glossy.

4 Stir a third of the whites into the cooled chocolate mixture to lighten it, then pour the chocolate mixture over the remaining whites. Using a rubber spatula or large metal spoon, gently fold the sauce into the whites. (Don't worry about a few white streaks.) Spoon into the prepared dishes.

5 To make the white chocolate sauce, put the chopped white chocolate and the cream into a small saucepan. Place over low heat and cook, stirring constantly until melted and smooth. Remove from the heat and stir in the liqueur and orange rind, then pour into a serving pitcher and keep warm.

6 Bake the soufflés for 10–12 minutes until risen and set, but still slightly wobbly in the center. Dust with confectioners' sugar and decorate with a sprig of red currants and a white chocolate rose. Serve the sauce separately.

Bitter Chocolate Mousse

This is the quintessential French dessert– easy to prepare ahead, rich and extremely delicious. Use the darkest chocolate you can find for the most authentic and intense chocolate flavor.

INGREDIENTS

Serves 8

8 ounces semisweet chocolate, chopped

2 tablespoons orange liqueur or brandy

2 tablespoons unsalted butter, cut into small pieces

4 eggs, separated

6 tablespoons whipping cream

¼ teaspoon cream of tartar

3 tablespoons superfine sugar

crème fraîche or sour cream and chocolate curls, to decorate

1 Place the chocolate and ¼ cup of water in a heavy saucepan. Melt over low heat, stirring until smooth. Remove the pan from the heat and whisk in the orange liqueur and butter.

2 With an electric mixer, beat the egg yolks for 2–3 minutes, until thick and creamy, then slowly beat into the melted chocolate until well blended. Set aside.

3 Whip the cream until soft peaks form and stir a spoonful into the chocolate to lighten it. Fold in the remaining cream.

4 In a clean, grease-free bowl, using an electric mixer, beat the egg whites until frothy. Add the cream of tartar and continue beating until they form soft peaks. Gradually sprinkle on the sugar and continue beating until the whites are stiff and glossy.

5 Using a rubber spatula or large metal spoon, stir one-quarter of the egg whites into the chocolate mixture, then gently fold in the remaining whites, cutting down to the bottom, along the sides and up to the top in a semicircular motion until they are just combined. (Don't worry about a few white streaks.) Gently spoon into an 8-cup dish or into eight individual dishes. Chill for at least 2 hours, until set and chilled.

6 Spoon a little crème fraîche or sour cream over the mousse and decorate with chocolate curls.

Mocha Cream Pots

The name of this rich baked custard, a classic French dessert, comes from the baking cups, called pots de crème. *The addition of coffee gives the dessert an exotic touch.*

INGREDIENTS

Serves 8

1 tablespoon instant coffee powder

2 cups milk

⅓ cup superfine sugar

8 ounces semisweet chocolate, chopped

2 teaspoons vanilla extract

2 tablespoons coffee liqueur (optional)

7 egg yolks

whipped cream and crystallized violets, to decorate (optional)

1 Preheat the oven to 325°F. Place eight ½-cup *pots de crème* cups or ramekins in a roasting pan.

2 Put the instant coffee into a saucepan and stir in the milk, then add the sugar and set the pan over medium-high heat. Bring to a boil, stirring constantly, until the coffee and sugar have dissolved.

3 Remove the pan from the heat and add the chocolate. Stir until the chocolate has melted and the sauce is smooth. Stir in the vanilla extract and coffee liqueur, if using.

4 In a bowl, whisk the egg yolks to blend them lightly. Slowly whisk in the chocolate mixture until well blended, then strain the mixture into a pitcher and divide equally among the cups or ramekins. Place them in a roasting pan and pour in enough boiling water to come halfway up the sides of the cups or ramekins. Cover the pan with foil.

5 Bake for 30–35 minutes, until the custard is just set and a knife inserted into a custard comes out clean. Remove the cups or ramekins from the roasting pan and let cool. Place on a baking sheet, cover and chill completely. Decorate with the whipped cream and crystallized violets, if using.

Tiramisù

"Tiramisù" is Italian for "pick me up," and this rich egg and coffee dessert does just that!

INGREDIENTS

Serves 6–8

1¼ pounds mascarpone

5 eggs, separated, at room temperature

½ cup superfine sugar

pinch of salt

ladyfingers, to line dish(es)

½ cup strong espresso coffee

¼ cup brandy or rum (optional)

unsweetened cocoa powder, to sprinkle

1 Beat the mascarpone in a small bowl until soft. In a separate bowl beat the egg yolks with the sugar (reserving 1 tablespoon), until the mixture is pale yellow and fluffy. Gradually beat in the softened mascarpone.

2 Using an electric beater or wire whisk, beat the egg whites with the salt until they form stiff peaks. Fold the egg whites into the mascarpone mixture.

3 Line one large or 6–8 individual serving dishes with the ladyfingers. Add the reserved sugar to the coffee, and stir in the brandy, if using.

4 Sprinkle the coffee over the ladyfingers. They should be moist but not saturated. Cover with half of the egg mixture. Make another layer of ladyfingers moistened with coffee, and cover with the remaining egg mixture. Sprinkle with cocoa powder. Chill for at least 1 hour, preferably more, before serving.

Zabaglione

This airy Italian egg custard fortified with sweet wine is usually eaten warm with cookies or fruit.

INGREDIENTS

Serves 3–4

3 egg yolks

3 tablespoons superfine sugar

5 tablespoons marsala or white dessert wine

pinch of grated orange rind

1 In the top half of a heavy boiler, or in a heatproof bowl away from the heat, whisk the egg yolks with the sugar until pale yellow. Beat in the marsala.

2 Place the pan or bowl over a pan of simmering water, and continue whisking until the custard is a frothy, light mass and evenly coats the back of a spoon, 6–8 minutes. Do not let the upper container touch the hot water, or the zabaglione may curdle.

3 Stir in the orange rind. Serve immediately.

COOK'S TIP

A scant teaspoon of ground cinnamon may be added.

Chocolate Profiteroles

This mouthwatering dessert is served in cafés throughout France. Sometimes the profiteroles are filled with whipped cream instead of ice cream, but they are always drizzled with chocolate sauce.

Serves 4–6

10 ounces semisweet chocolate

3 cups vanilla ice cream

For the profiteroles

¾ cup all-purpose flour

¼ teaspoon salt

pinch of freshly grated nutmeg

6 tablespoons unsalted butter, cut into
   6 pieces

3 eggs

1 Preheat the oven to 400°F and butter a baking sheet.

2 To make the profiteroles, sift together the flour, salt and nutmeg. In a medium saucepan, bring the butter and ¾ cup water to a boil. Remove from the heat and add the dry ingredients all at once. Beat with a wooden spoon for about 1 minute, until well blended and the mixture starts to pull away from the sides of the pan, then set the pan over low heat and cook the mixture for about 2 minutes, beating constantly. Remove from the heat.

3 Beat one egg in a small bowl and set aside. Add the remaining eggs, one at a time, to the flour mixture, beating well. Add the beaten egg gradually, until the dough is smooth and shiny; it should fall slowly when dropped from a spoon.

4 Using a tablespoon, drop the dough onto the baking sheet in 12 mounds. Bake for 25–30 minutes, until the pastry is well risen and browned. Turn off the oven and let the puffs cool with the oven door open.

5 To make the sauce, place the chocolate and ½ cup warm water in a double boiler or in a bowl and melt, stirring occasionally, over a pan of hot water.

6 Split the profiteroles in half and put a small scoop of ice cream in each. Arrange on a serving platter. Pour the sauce over the top and serve immediately.

Tarte Tatin

This upside-down apple tart was first made by two sisters who served it in their restaurant in the Loire Valley in France.

Serves 8–10

8 ounces puff or pie pastry

10–12 large Golden Delicious apples

lemon juice

½ cup butter, cut into pieces

½ cup superfine sugar

½ teaspoon ground cinnamon

crème fraîche or whipped cream, to serve

1 On a lightly floured surface, roll out the pastry into an 11-inch round less than ¼ inch thick. Transfer to a lightly floured baking sheet and chill.

2 Peel the apples, cut them in half lengthwise and core. Sprinkle them generously with lemon juice.

3 Preheat the oven to 450°F. In a 10-inch cast-iron pan, cook the butter, sugar and cinnamon over medium heat until the butter has melted and the sugar dissolved, stirring occasionally. Continue cooking for 6–8 minutes, until the mixture turns a medium caramel color, then remove the pan from the heat and arrange the apple halves, standing on their edges, in the pan, fitting them in tightly since they shrink during cooking.

4 Return the apple-filled pan to the heat and bring to a simmer over medium heat for 20–25 minutes until the apples are tender and colored. Remove the tin from the heat and cool slightly.

5 Place the pastry on top of the apple-filled pan and tuck the edges of the pastry inside the edge of the pan around the apples.

6 Pierce the pastry in two or three places, then bake for 25–30 minutes, until the pastry is golden and the filling is bubbling. Let the tart cool in the pan for 10–15 minutes.

7 To serve, run a sharp knife around the edge of the pan to loosen the pastry. Cover with a serving plate and, holding them tightly, carefully invert the pan and plate together (do this over the sink in case any caramel drips). Lift off the pan and loosen any apples that stick with a spatula. Serve the tart warm with cream.

Greek Chocolate Mousse Tartlets

The combination of white chocolate and plain yogurt makes a delicious and light, but not too sweet, filling.

Serves 6

1½ cups all-purpose flour

2 tablespoons cocoa powder

2 tablespoons confectioners' sugar

½ cup butter

melted dark chocolate, to decorate

For the filling

7 ounces white chocolate, broken into
    squares

½ cup milk

2 teaspoons powdered gelatin

2 tablespoons superfine sugar

1 teaspoon vanilla extract

2 eggs, separated

generous 1 cup plain yogurt

1 Preheat the oven to 375°F. Sift the flour, cocoa and confectioners' sugar into a bowl.

2 Place the butter in a pan with ¼ cup water and heat gently until just melted. Cool, then stir into the flour to make a smooth dough. Chill until firm.

3 Roll out the pastry and line six deep, 4-inch loose-bottomed tart pans.

4 Prick the bottom of each pastry shell all over with a fork, cover with waxed paper weighed down with baking beans and bake blind for 10 minutes. Remove the baking beans and paper, return to the oven and bake another 15 minutes, or until the pastry is firm. Let cool in the pans.

5 Make the filling. Melt the chocolate in a heatproof bowl over hot water. Pour the milk into a saucepan, sprinkle on the gelatin and heat gently, stirring, until the gelatin has dissolved completely. Remove from the heat and stir in the chocolate.

6 Whisk the sugar, vanilla extract and egg yolks in a large bowl, then beat in the chocolate mixture. Beat in the yogurt until evenly mixed.

7 Whisk the egg whites in a clean, grease-free bowl until stiff, then fold into the mixture. Divide among the pastry shells and let set.

8 Drizzle the melted dark chocolate over the tartlets to decorate.

Chestnut Pudding

This is an Italian specialty, made during the months of October and November when fresh sweet chestnuts are gathered.

INGREDIENTS

Serves 4–5

1 pound fresh sweet chestnuts

1¼ cups milk

½ cup superfine sugar

2 eggs, separated, at room temperature

¼ cup unsweetened cocoa powder

½ teaspoon pure vanilla extract

½ cup confectioners' sugar, sifted

fresh whipped cream, to garnish

marrons glacés, to garnish

1 Cut a cross in the sides of the chestnuts, and drop them into a pan of boiling water. Cook for 5–6 minutes. Remove with a slotted spoon, and peel while still warm.

2 Place the peeled chestnuts in a heavy or nonstick saucepan with the milk and half of the superfine sugar. Cook over low heat, stirring occasionally, until soft. Remove from the heat and let cool. Press the contents of the pan through a strainer.

3 Preheat the oven to 350°F. Beat the egg yolks with the remaining superfine sugar until the mixture is pale yellow and fluffy. Beat in the cocoa powder and the vanilla.

4 In a separate bowl, whisk the egg whites with a wire whisk or electric beater until they form soft peaks. Gradually beat in the sifted confectioners' sugar and continue beating until the mixture forms stiff peaks.

5 Fold the chestnut and egg yolk mixtures together. Fold in the egg whites. Transfer the mixture to one large or several individual buttered pudding molds. Place on a baking sheet, and bake in the oven for 12–20 minutes, depending on the size. Remove from the oven, and let cool for 10 minutes before unmolding. Serve garnished with whipped cream and marrons glacés.

Coffee Granita

A granita is a cross between a frozen drink and a flavored ice, very popular in Italy. The consistency should be slushy, not solid. It can be made at home with the help of a food processor.

INGREDIENTS

Serves 4–5

½ cup granulated sugar

1 cup very strong espresso coffee, cooled

whipped cream, to garnish (optional)

1 Heat 2 cups water with the sugar over low heat until the sugar dissolves. Bring to a boil. Remove from the heat and let cool.

2 Combine the coffee with the sugar syrup. Place in a shallow container or ice tray, and freeze until solid. Plunge the bottom of the frozen container or tray in very hot water for a few seconds. Turn the frozen mixture out, and chop it into large chunks.

3 Place the mixture in a food processor fitted with a metal blade, and process until it forms small crystals. Spoon into serving glasses and top with whipped cream, if desired. If you do not plan on serving the granita immediately, pour the processed mixture back into a shallow container or ice tray and freeze until serving time. Let thaw for a few minutes before serving, or process again.

Lemon Granita

Nothing is more refreshing on a hot summer's day than a cooling lemon granita.

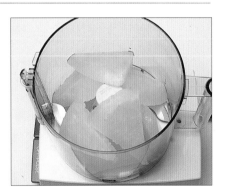

INGREDIENTS

Serves 4–5

½ cup granulated sugar

grated rind of 1 lemon, scrubbed
    before grating

juice of 2 large lemons

1 Heat 2 cups water with the sugar over low heat until the sugar dissolves. Bring to a boil. Remove from the heat, and let cool.

2 Combine the lemon rind and juice with the sugar syrup. Place in a shallow container or ice tray, and freeze until solid.

3 Plunge the bottom of the frozen container or tray in very hot water for a few seconds. Turn the frozen mixture out, and chop it into chunks.

4 Place the mixture in a food processor fitted with a metal blade, and process until it forms small crystals. Spoon into individual serving glasses.

Peach Melba

The story that one of the great French chefs, Auguste Escoffier, created this dessert in honor of the opera singer Nellie Melba, is now forever enshrined in culinary, if not musical, history.

INGREDIENTS

Serves 6

¼ cup superfine sugar

1 vanilla bean, split lengthwise

3 large peaches

For the sauce

2⅔ cups fresh or frozen raspberries

1 tablespoon lemon juice

2–3 tablespoons superfine sugar

2–3 tablespoons raspberry liqueur
    (optional)

vanilla ice cream, to serve

fresh mint leaves and fresh raspberries, to
    decorate (optional)

1 In a saucepan large enough to hold the peach halves in a single layer, combine 4 cups water with the sugar and vanilla bean. Bring to a boil over medium heat, stirring occasionally, to dissolve the sugar.

2 Cut the peaches in half and twist the halves to separate them. Using a small teaspoon, remove the peach pits. Add the peach halves to the poaching syrup, cut-sides down, adding more water, if needed, to cover the fruit. Press a piece of waxed paper against the surface, reduce the heat to medium-low, then cover and simmer for 12–15 minutes until tender – the time will depend on the ripeness of the fruit. Remove the pan from the heat and let the peaches cool in the syrup.

3 Remove the peaches from the syrup and peel off the skins. Place on several thicknesses of paper towels to drain (reserve the syrup for another use), then cover and chill.

4 Put the raspberries, lemon juice and sugar in a blender or food processor fitted with the metal blade. Process for 1 minute, scraping down the sides once. Press through a fine sieve into a small bowl, then stir in the raspberry liqueur, if using, and put in the fridge to chill.

5 To serve, place a peach half, cut-side up, on a dessert plate, fill with a scoop of vanilla ice cream and spoon the raspberry sauce over the ice cream. Decorate with mint leaves and a few fresh raspberries, if using.

Australian Hazelnut Pavlova

Meringue topped with fresh fruit and cream – perfect for summer dinner parties.

Serves 4–6

3 egg whites

generous ¾ cup superfine sugar

1 teaspoon cornstarch

1 teaspoon white wine vinegar

5 tablespoons chopped roasted hazelnuts

1 cup heavy cream

1 tablespoon orange juice

2 tablespoons plain thick and creamy
   yogurt

2 ripe nectarines, pitted and sliced

1⅓ cups raspberries

1–2 tablespoons red currant jelly, warmed

1 Preheat the oven to 275°F. Lightly grease a baking sheet. Draw an 8-inch circle on a sheet of waxed paper. Place pencil-side down on the baking sheet.

2 Place the egg whites in a clean, grease-free bowl and whisk with an electric mixer until stiff. Whisk in the sugar 1 tablespoon at a time, whisking well after each addition.

3 Add the cornstarch, vinegar and hazelnuts and fold in carefully with a large metal spoon.

4 Spoon the meringue onto the marked circle and spread out, making a depression in the center.

5 Bake for about 1¼–1½ hours, until crisp. Let cool, then transfer to a serving platter.

6 Whip the cream and orange juice until just thick, stir in the yogurt and spoon onto the meringue. Top with the fruit and drizzle with the red currant jelly. Serve immediately.

Lemon Ricotta Cake

This lemony cake from Sardinia is quite different from a traditional cheesecake.

INGREDIENTS

Serves 6–8

6 tablespoons butter

¾ cup granulated sugar

generous ⅓ cup ricotta cheese

3 eggs, separated

1½ cups all-purpose flour

grated rind of 1 lemon

3 tablespoons fresh lemon juice

1½ teaspoons baking powder

confectioners' sugar, for dusting

1 Grease a 9-inch round cake or springform pan. Line the bottom with waxed paper. Grease the paper. Dust with flour. Set aside. Preheat the oven to 350°F.

2 Cream the butter and sugar together until smooth. Beat in the ricotta cheese.

3 Beat in the egg yolks, one at a time. Add 2 tablespoons of the flour and the lemon rind and juice. Sift the baking powder into the remaining flour and beat into the batter until just blended.

4 Beat the egg whites until they form stiff peaks. Fold them carefully into the batter.

5 Transfer the mixture to the prepared pan. Bake for 45 minutes, or until a cake tester inserted in the center of the cake comes out clean. Let the cake cool in the pan for 10 minutes before turning it out onto a rack to cool. Dust the cake generously with confectioners' sugar before serving.

Peaches with Amaretti Stuffing

Peaches are plentiful all over Italy. They are sometimes prepared hot, as in this classic dish.

INGREDIENTS

Serves 4

4 ripe fresh peaches

juice of ½ lemon

⅔ cup amaretti or almond cookies, crushed

2 tablespoons marsala, brandy or peach brandy

2 tablespoons butter, at room temperature

½ teaspoon vanilla extract

2 tablespoons granulated sugar

1 egg yolk

1 Preheat the oven to 350°F. Wash the peaches. Cut them in half and remove the pits. Enlarge the hollow left by the pits by scooping out some of the peach with a small spoon. Sprinkle the peach halves with the lemon juice.

2 Soften the amaretti crumbs in the marsala for a few minutes. Beat the butter until soft. Stir in the amaretti mixture with all the remaining ingredients.

3 Arrange the peach halves in a baking dish in one layer, hollow side upward. Divide the amaretti mixture into 8 parts, and fill the hollows, mounding the stuffing up in the center. Bake for 35–40 minutes. These are delicious served hot or cold.

Bread Pudding with Pecans

A version of the British classic deliciously flavored with pecans and orange rind.

INGREDIENTS

Serves 6

1⅔ cups milk

1⅔ cups light cream or half-and-half

¾ cup superfine sugar

3 eggs, beaten to mix

2 teaspoons grated orange rind

1 teaspoon vanilla extract

24 slices of day-old French bread, ½-inch thick

½ cup toasted pecans, chopped

confectioners' sugar, for sprinkling

whipped or sour cream and maple syrup, to serve

1 Put 1½ cups each of the milk and cream in a saucepan. Add the sugar. Warm over low heat, stirring to dissolve the sugar. Remove from the heat and cool. Add the eggs, orange rind and vanilla and mix well.

2 Arrange half of the bread slices in a buttered 9–10-inch baking dish. Sprinkle two-thirds of the pecans over the bread. Arrange the remaining bread slices on top and scatter on the rest of the pecans.

3 Pour the egg mixture evenly over the bread slices. Soak for 30 minutes. Press the top layer of bread down into the liquid once or twice.

4 Preheat the oven to 350°F. If the top layer of bread slices looks dry and all the liquid has been absorbed, moisten with the remaining milk and cream.

5 Set the baking dish in a roasting pan. Add enough water to the pan to come halfway up the sides of the dish. Bring the water to a boil.

6 Transfer to the oven. Bake for 40 minutes or until the pudding is set and golden brown on top. Sprinkle the top of the pudding with sifted confectioners' sugar and serve warm, with whipped or sour cream and maple syrup, if desired.

Spiced Peach Crisp

The topping of this classic dessert has rolled oats for extra crunchiness.

INGREDIENTS

Serves 6

3 pounds ripe but firm peaches, peeled, pitted and sliced

¼ cup superfine sugar

½ teaspoon ground cinnamon

1 teaspoon lemon juice

whipped cream or vanilla ice cream, for serving (optional)

For the topping

1 cup all-purpose flour

¼ teaspoon ground cinnamon

¼ teaspoon ground allspice

1 cup rolled oats

¾ cup light brown sugar

8 tablespoons butter

1 Preheat the oven to 375°F. For the topping, sift the flour and spices into a bowl. Add the oats and sugar and stir to combine. Cut or rub in the butter until the mixture resembles coarse crumbs.

2 Toss the peaches with the sugar, cinnamon and lemon juice. Put the fruit mixture in an 8- or 9-inch diameter baking dish.

3 Sprinkle the topping over the fruit in an even layer. Bake for 30–35 minutes. Serve warm, with whipped cream or vanilla ice cream, if desired.

VARIATION

Use apricots or nectarines instead of peaches. Substitute nutmeg for the cinnamon.

Jam Tart

Jam tarts are popular in Italy where they are traditionally decorated with pastry strips.

Serves 6–8

1¾ cups all-purpose flour

pinch of salt

¼ cup granulated sugar

½ cup butter or margarine, chilled

1 egg

¼ teaspoon grated lemon rind

1¼ cups fruit jam, such as raspberry, apricot or strawberry

1 egg, lightly beaten with 2 tablespoons whipping cream, for glazing

1 Make the pastry by placing the flour, salt and sugar in a mixing bowl. Using a pastry blender or two knives, cut the butter into the dry ingredients as quickly as possible until the mixture resembles coarse crumbs.

2 Beat the egg with the lemon rind in a cup, and pour it over the flour mixture. Combine with a fork until the dough holds together. If it is too crumbly, mix in 1–2 tablespoons of water.

3 Gather the dough into two balls, one slightly larger than the other, and flatten into circles. Wrap in waxed paper, and put in the fridge for at least 40 minutes.

4 Lightly grease a shallow 9-inch tart or pie pan, preferably with a removable bottom. Roll out the larger circle of pastry on a lightly floured surface to a thickness of about ⅛ inch.

5 Roll the pastry around the rolling pin and transfer to the prepared pan. Trim the edges evenly with a small knife. Prick the bottom with a fork. Chill for at least 30 minutes.

6 Preheat the oven to 375°F. Spread the jam thickly and evenly over the bottom of the pastry. Roll out the remaining pastry.

7 Cut the pastry into strips about ½ inch wide using a ruler as a guide. Arrange them over the jam in a lattice pattern. Trim the edges of the strips even with the edge of the pan, pressing them lightly onto the pastry shell. Brush the pastry with the egg and cream glaze. Bake for about 35 minutes or until the pastry is golden brown. Let cool before serving.

Indian Ice Cream (Kulfi)

Kulfi-wallahs (ice cream vendors) have always made kulfi, and continue to this day, without using modern freezers. Try this method – it works extremely well in an ordinary freezer. You will need to start making kulfi the day before you want to serve it.

INGREDIENTS

Serves 4–6

3 cans (14 ounces each) evaporated milk

3 egg whites, whisked until peaks form

3 cups confectioners' sugar

1 teaspoon ground cardamom

1 tablespoon rose water

1½ cups pistachios, chopped

generous ½ cup golden raisins

¾ cup sliced almonds

2 tablespoons candied cherries, halved

1 Remove the labels from the cans of evaporated milk and put the cans down in a pan with a tight-fitting cover. Fill the pan with water to reach three-quarters up the cans. Bring to a boil, cover and simmer for 20 minutes. When cool, remove and chill the cans in the fridge for 24 hours.

2 Open the cans and empty the milk into a large, chilled bowl. Whisk until it doubles in quantity, then fold in the whisked egg whites and confectioners' sugar.

3 Gently fold in the remaining ingredients, seal the bowl with plastic wrap and leave in the freezer for 1 hour.

4 Remove the ice cream from the freezer and mix well with a fork. Transfer to a freezer container and return to the freezer for a final setting. Remove from the freezer 10 minutes before serving in scoops.

Spiced Mexican Fritters

Hot, sweet and spicy fritters are popular in both Spain and Mexico for either breakfast or a snack.

INGREDIENTS

Makes 16 (serves 4)

1 cup raspberries

3 tablespoons confectioners' sugar

3 tablespoons orange juice

For the fritters

¼ cup butter

⅔ cup all-purpose flour, sifted

2 eggs, lightly beaten

1 tablespoon ground almonds

corn oil, for frying

1 tablespoon confectioners' sugar and
    ½ teaspoon ground cinnamon, for dusting

8 fresh raspberries, to decorate

1 Mash the raspberries with the confectioners' sugar, and push through a sieve into a bowl to remove the seeds. Stir in the orange juice and chill until ready to serve.

2 To make the fritters, place the butter and ⅔ cup water in a saucepan and heat gently until the butter has melted. Bring to a boil and, when boiling, add the sifted flour all at once and turn off the heat.

3 Beat until the mixture leaves the sides of the pan and forms a ball. Cool slightly, then beat in the eggs a little at a time, then add the almonds.

4 Spoon the mixture into a pastry bag fitted with a large star nozzle. Half-fill a saucepan or deep-fat fryer with the oil and heat to 375°F.

5 Pipe about four 2-inch lengths at a time into the hot oil, cutting off the raw mixture with a knife as you go. Deep-fry for about 3–4 minutes, turning occasionally, until puffed up and golden. Drain on paper towels and keep warm in the oven while frying the remainder.

6 When you have fried all the mixture, dust the hot fritters with confectioners' sugar and cinnamon. Serve three or four per person on serving plates drizzled with the raspberry sauce, dust again with sifted confectioners' sugar and decorate with fresh raspberries.

Thai Fried Bananas

A very simple and quick Thai pudding – bananas fried in butter, brown sugar and lime juice, and sprinkled with toasted coconut.

INGREDIENTS

Serves 4

3 tablespoons butter

4 large slightly underripe bananas

1 tablespoon shredded coconut

¼ cup light brown sugar

¼ cup lime juice

2 fresh lime slices, to decorate

thick and creamy plain yogurt, to serve

1 Heat the butter in a large frying pan or wok and fry the bananas for 1–2 minutes on each side, or until they are lightly golden in color.

2 Meanwhile, dry-fry the coconut in a small frying pan until lightly browned, and reserve.

3 Sprinkle the sugar into the pan with the bananas, add the lime juice and cook, stirring, until dissolved. Arrange the bananas on a serving dish. Sprinkle the coconut over the bananas, decorate with lime slices and serve with the thick and creamy yogurt.

Index